FROMFATHERTOSON

SHOWING YOUR BOY HOW TO WALK WITH CHRIST

CHAP CLARK

NAVPRESS

Bringing Truth to Life
P.O. Box 35001, Colorado Springs, Colorado 80935

OUR GUARANTEE TO YOU

The Navigators is an international Christian organization. Our mission is to reach, disciple, and equip people to know Christ and to make Him known through successive generations. We envision multitudes of diverse people in the United States and every other nation who have a passionate love for Christ, live a lifestyle of sharing Christ's love, and multiply spiritual laborers among those without Christ.

NavPress is the publishing ministry of The Navigators. NavPress publications help believers learn biblical truth and apply what they learn to their lives and ministries. Our mission is to stimulate spiritual formation among our readers.

© 2002 by Chap Clark
All rights reserved. No part of this publication may be reproduced in any form without written permission from NavPress, P.O. Box 35001, Colorado Springs, CO 80935.
www.navpress.com

ISBN 1-57683-294-5

Cover design by Dan Jamison
Cover photo © Corbis Corporation/The Stock Market/LWA/Dann Tordif/2002
Creative Team: Brad Lewis, Amy Spencer, Pat Miller

Some of the anecdotal illustrations in this book are true to life and are included with the permission of the persons involved. All other illustrations are composites of real situations, and any resemblance to people living or dead is coincidental.

Unless otherwise identified, all Scripture quotations in this publication are taken from the HOLY BIBLE: NEW INTERNATIONAL VERSION® (NIV®). Copyright © 1973, 1978, 1984 by International Bible Society. Used by permission of Zondervan Publishing House. All rights reserved. Other versions used include *The Message: New Testament with Psalms and Proverbs* (MSG) by Eugene H. Peterson, copyright © 1993, 1994, 1995, used by permission of NavPress Publishing Group; and the *New Revised Standard Version* (NRSV), copyright © 1989, by the Division of Christian Education of the National Council of the Churches of Christ in the USA, used by permission, all rights reserved.

Clark, Chap, 1954-
　From father to son : showing your boy how to walk with Christ / Chap Clark.
　　p. cm.
Includes bibliographical references.
　ISBN 1-57683-294-5
　1. Fathers and sons--Religious aspects--Christianity. I. Title.
　BV4529.17 .C57 2002
　248.8'421--dc21
　　　　　　　　　　　　　　2002007019

Printed in the United States of America

1 2 3 4 5 6 7 8 9 10 / 06 05 04 03 02

FOR A FREE CATALOG OF
NAVPRESS BOOKS & BIBLE STUDIES,
CALL 1-800-366-7788 (USA)
OR 1-416-499-4615 (CANADA)

CONTENTS

ACKNOWLEDGMENTS

LIKE ANY BOOK, THIS ONE IS A PRODUCT OF SEVERAL PEOPLE; I just got to write it. I have believed for years that anything I have to offer is due to the cumulative influence of God and others who have loved me.

I've been married to Dee for more than two decades, and every year gets richer and more exciting than the year before. Her belief in me, her putting up with those days when I whine, and her unending compassion for me provide tangible strength to keep me following my Lord.

Our boys, Chap and Rob, whom I use a little too often in this book, are such shining stars to me. Each is unique, yet they both have always had an amazing ability to teach me where I need to grow as a man, a husband, and a dad. But as they're growing, I especially appreciate the foundation we've built, and I look forward to years of walking on the journey with Christ together.

Though this book is about sons, this one is also for Katie, our "Angel Eyes." In a previous book, *Daughters and Dads,* Dee and I somehow failed to mention her. But not now, Katie, for you have proven to me that we Christian men are the losers when we don't see that God wants us to connect with our daughters every bit as much as we do with our sons. You bring me wisdom and great joy.

There have also been many great friends who have walked along the journey with me. Jim, Jeff, and Ralph— thanks for reading the first draft; you were invaluable. Our Glendale couple's group: Nancy and Wardie, Angela and Jim, Judy and Ralph, Meredith and Rusty, and Annie and

Dave—thanks for the committed friendship that keeps me going. And Billy and Brad, you guys are the best!

Thanks, too, to my students and colleagues at Fuller Theological Seminary: You all teach me to keep pushing the envelope on what it means to follow Jesus Christ. As you know, I'll never be satisfied with what "everybody" says, but only in where the Spirit leads us. You've helped me continue on that road.

This book could not have been written without the love, guidance, modeling, and influence of my parents—John and Gale Clark, and John and Jan Carlson (Dee's folks). Because of what you have taught me and how you have loved me, with great patience and support, I am able to pass that on to my boys.

FROM FATHER TO SON:
LEADING THE WAY

THIS BOOK ISN'T MEANT TO BE READ ALONE. SURE, IT CAN STILL make a difference if you read it during a break at work or late at night in bed. But the issue of fathering and the ways I've attempted to redefine the task of leading your son to a deep and rich relationship with Christ are far better explored with a few other guys. I recommend that this book be read in a group of dads, perhaps taking a chapter a week and then getting together over breakfast to explore, discuss, and even argue the implications of each chapter. I promise that at least some of what you read here will be new, maybe even controversial. Getting together with a group of men struggling through the same issues will make a long-term difference in the kind of father you are and will become. If you don't already meet with a group on a somewhat regular basis, use this book as a catalyst to start living in the kind of relational intimacy God has designed for each of us. Grab some guys and start the journey!

However, before you get too far in this book, I have to let you in on something. In many ways, I have no business writing a book like this. None.

I'm the dad of two young men: a twenty-year-old and a seventeen-year-old (as well as a fourteen-year-old girl— another topic entirely). As a father for the last twenty-plus years, I've dreamed, prayed, cajoled, argued, devised, deceived, spied, fought, cried, yelled, and compromised in order to somehow (a) train up my boys in the way they should go (see Proverbs 22:6) and (b) let them know that I long to be the very best father to them I possibly can be. In so many ways, I have failed miserably.

Sure, on a good day, both of my sons will tell you that as dads go I'm near the top of the list—a bit strict, perhaps, but basically a good guy who tries hard. But with very little coaxing, each could also launch into talking about times and situations where I behaved as if I needed to be locked away somewhere for intense parental training and indoctrination.

It's ironic how my dreams, plans, and expectations have so dramatically shifted after all these years. When Chap Jr. was born, no one could have told me that I would be anything less than the prototypical father for the new millennium. When Rob came along, the vision expanded to include images of the three of us in joint ministry, of long walks detailing world-changing strategies, and of two compliant but strong-in-their-own-right sons who would dutifully follow in my footsteps for a season but soon "carry my torch" into the decades beyond me. Yet gradually, and without much reflection, my dreams turned south, and I realized that neither one was a clone of me, nor should he be. Accompanying this process was the inevitable and universal disappointment of fatherhood— I'm not the father I dreamed I'd be. They pushed buttons in me I didn't know existed. I learned how to lord my authority over them to get my own way. I was disappointed and angry when they didn't live up to my ideal or expectations.

I have been, in many ways, a disaster as a dad.

That's the dark side. But in many ways, I've been a good, and occasionally great, father to my sons. I've cried with and for them. I've been a fan and (generally) an available friend. I've given them space to be themselves and opportunities to explore life the way they see fit. I've cared for them with passion and compassion, with fear and trembling, and with every fiber of my being.

This is precisely what you need to know about me and

about the task of fathering as you approach taking your son into the turbulent, wild waters of the faith journey. If you haven't figured this out yet, listen carefully: In the final analysis, nobody's any good at being the perfect father—*nobody!*

Sure, some families and dads *look* as though they have this thing wired. But that image is often sustained and perpetuated more by temperament and family structure and system than by what the fathers actually *do* or have control over.

Here's why this point is so crucial: you're just like *every other guy* trying to be the best father possible for your boy. You'll be a great dad now and then, a good father sometimes, and an out-of-control goofball every once in a while.

This is a book by a normal, fallible father for other normal, fallible fathers. It's a book about *real* Christian faith in a *real* world—the world you and your son live in. It's a handbook on the essence of what it means to raise up your son as a follower of Jesus Christ in a very difficult and antagonistic cultural climate. I am not and do not pretend to be an expert on fathering, because every expert I know stinks at some aspect of the task. *Nobody* is an "expert" at fathering, because far too many complexities and moving pieces exist when it comes to raising kids in a postmodern, fragmented, helter-skelter world. I've studied a great deal about fathering, I know how the process is initiated, and I *generally* understand what fathers need to do to bring out the best in their sons. But in the end, I'm just one father on the journey, sharing some insights with other men who care about their sons.

So I invite you to continue on this journey with eyes wide open to what God would have for you and your son. Pray as you go. Find a few guys to walk with you as you deal with the issues I bring up. In each chapter I've given you questions for group discussion, and a few "baby steps" to help you implement the issues brought up in the chapter. These aren't final answers by any means—they're just tools and ideas to help you on the journey with your son.

Most of all, be encouraged. I have no illusions that this is easy, simple, or even "works." Don't go into this looking for the single magic formula that will ensure your son's consistent faith. But do expect God to whisper his encouragement and some specific insights into your heart as you seek to be the very best dad your son could ever hope for.

Chap Clark
La Canada, California

PART 1

FROM FATHER TO SON:
THE TASK OF DISCIPLESHIP

What We Shoot For:
Creating the Environment for Lifelong Faith

Every time you listen with great attentiveness to the voice
that calls you the Beloved, you will discover within yourself a desire to hear that voice longer and more deeply. It
is like discovering a well in the desert. Once you have
touched wet ground, you want to dig deeper.

—HENRI NOUWEN

REMEMBER THE *ANDY GRIFFITH SHOW?* THE OPENING FEATURED
Sheriff Andy walking along a dirt road with his son,
fishing rods in hand. This was the quintessential picture of
the perfect father-son duo, together enjoying the bliss of
the God-given institution of fatherhood.

What father doesn't want that same kind of intimate
relationship with his son? And what Christian father doesn't
long for a deep, real, warm *spiritual* relationship with his
son? When a son is born, a dad dreams of the times they'll
have together—taking walks, fishing or hiking, talking
about life and faith and love.

But then something begins to squeeze out the eupho-
ria of these dreams. Around eleven or twelve, the boy

begins to have his own interests, skills, and dreams. He becomes less interested in the things dad wants to do and discuss, and he begins to move from ally to adversary. Except for when father and son share superficial social sedatives like sports and hobbies, the boy is increasingly bored and distant when it comes to any kind of input or leadership from his dad. And as he enters the middle adolescent years and prepares to leave home to become a man, most often the father-son bond is cordial at best, with some warm memories and patterns perhaps, but with a distance that both sense but neither can easily name. Then he leaves and the dad ponders the loss of a friend who never really was.

In most families, this is frighteningly normal. But it doesn't have to be that way. At times, your adolescent son will show openness to a relationship with you, but it will have to be on his terms, at his bidding. You can't schedule a time of intimate connection with your son—those days are long past. You can't even control when he'll be receptive to investing in a dialogue about God and faith and spiritual growth.

In today's world, adolescence is a drawn-out and complex journey, and your son will do whatever he can to figure out how to navigate the bumps, twists, and turns along the way. He needs you in his life. For almost every situation, he wants you. But as the dad, you must figure out what it means to love and lead your son into a meaningful life centered on a deep, powerful relationship with God.

This section is about the environment your son needs in order to be able to grow up into Christ. It's about surveying the territory, laying the stakes, and digging the well with him. It's about teaching him how to find water for his soul and how to tap into the richness a relationship with God brings. And it's about knowing and then passing on to him the essential elements of the task of lifelong discipleship. You're the guide, the friend. But he must ultimately be the one to dig his own well. This section surveys the task of discipleship by looking at four marks of believers that prepare the way for our sons to dig the well of faith that will nourish them for the rest of their lives.

CHAPTER 1

THE TASK OF DISCIPLESHIP: SETTING THE COURSE

Since my youth, O God, you have taught me, and to this day I declare your marvelous deeds. Even when I am old and gray, do not forsake me, O God, till I declare your power to the next generation, your might to all who are to come.

—PSALM 71:17-18

WHAT DOES IT MEAN FOR A FATHER TO PASS FAITH ON TO HIS son? In working with young people for almost three decades, I've spent a lot of time trying to figure out what the "task" of passing on faith to the next generation really is. Of course, many books, philosophies, and definitions of "discipleship" have tried to uniquely and finally clarify the task. But passing on faith from one person to another across generations brings additional dynamics to the language of discipleship. What a son needs from his father is fluid and complex. He needs, first, a trusted model of authentic faith, and second, a father who knows what it means to create enough space for his son to grow up into the man God has called him to be.

THE ESSENCE OF ADOLESCENT DISCIPLESHIP

WHEN DEE AND I WERE YOUNG PARENTS, DESPERATE TO BRING UP our sons "in the training and instruction of the Lord"

(Ephesians 6:4), we grabbed any information we could get our hands on. We wanted to make sure we did the right thing as we raised our kids. But the older our boys got, the more we realized that, while some standard philosophies can apply in our parenting, our sons are unique. While short-term grounding worked great for one of our sons, it had exactly the opposite effect on the other. One needed to talk and understand where we were coming from, but the other wanted to quickly reconcile and move on. One is more a dreamer-lover; the other has a strong-willed, legal mind. Tips, techniques, and cookie-cutter formulas weren't the answer for our boys, and I suspect they're not the answer for yours.

I'm telling you this in case you're expecting this book to be another fill-in-the-blanks, follow the formula, how-to-type resource. I'm warning you now—this is *not* one of those books. Rather, it's a tool to help you define the tasks and parameters for bringing your son into a meaningful relationship with Jesus Christ. Yes, there are practical strategies and even a few programmatic specifics, but the bulk of this book is committed to helping dads know what it means to pass on faith to their sons. Actual "success" is defined here by how a father operates within the context of the issues of discipling a son, *not* by how quickly and observably his son lives the Christian life. That remains in the hands of the son and depends on his own relationship with God. We as fathers are simply called to model our faith, create an environment where faith can flourish, and walk with our sons on the journey.

Our attitude toward discipling our sons seems to have fallen victim to the instant messaging, on-the-fly e-mail, techno-gadget world that has seeped into our understanding and experience of faith. But neither parenting nor discipleship can be that easy or fast. Faith is an invitation to a wild, new journey. It can't be reduced to a secret now revealed or to six easy steps. It's a step-by-step daily walk with God, who promises to lead us.

A TRUSTED MODEL

IN A RAPIDLY CHANGING AND SOCIALLY EVOLVING WORLD, TWO unique yet related issues emerge that affect a father's ability to touch his son for Christ. First, cultural fragmentation has torn apart nearly every society. Different attitudes, commitments, and perceptions of reality between generations are just a sampling of many factors that can place a wedge between a father and his son. For example, consider the definition of "sex." For most Christian fathers, sex involves any intimate physical contact or fantasies about intimate contact. Most contemporary adults would acknowledge that a kiss or even holding hands can be a sexual expression. But not in today's adolescent world. Quite possibly, for your son, sex is intercourse; everything else is "just messing around." This is just one example of a world changing so rapidly that few of us can hope to keep up.

Many men offhandedly believe that the effects of cultural fragmentation aren't an issue for them and their sons. But I do believe this is a far wider and deeper problem than most dads recognize. You may *think* you know your son and his world and that you understand how he and his friends look at life. But I invite you to prayerfully consider that there's much about your son and his world that you know little or nothing about.

The second factor, which has been greatly influenced by the first, is the fact that adolescence lasts ten years longer than it did in the 1970s. Obviously, the reasons behind this are complex and varied, and it's not necessarily true for all kids. But most researchers agree that this stage in life that used to be completed around eighteen years of age now lasts well into the twenties and beyond for most kids. For many, it also begins earlier. Why? The majority opinion is that we have effectively dismantled many of the support systems that were designed to help children become adults. In our world, adults want to recapture their youth; kids see this and do not feel any rush to leave the freedoms they now enjoy.

This extended adolescence also influences a father's ability to impact his son for Jesus Christ. The kind of growth your son will probably experience is a slower, more frustrating, and less consistent journey than yours was. Only the rare father recognizes that development has changed and that kids today need far more time for authentic growth to occur. This impacts all aspects of the developmental journey—from relationships to identity to problem solving to conceptualization.

If you want to do a little firsthand research in this area, just check out the fifth-grade class at your local school. You'll notice that many of the girls look like they should be in high school, and the language and topics of conversation of both boys and girls are the stuff of R-rated movies. Then consider, on the other end of the adolescence spectrum, households who have children in their twenties (and even older) who are either living at home or are financially and emotionally dependent on their parents, perhaps coming back after college or even post-divorce in a renewed adolescence.

This culturally sanctioned extended adolescence means the road to maturity is long and winding. And it's more about baby steps and a slow, deliberate, inconsistent, and incremental process than a linear, neatly progressing "spiritual maturity" while your son is still in high school (or even college). This also means the bar of observable growth needs to be lowered to accommodate the realities of life in the new millennium. This isn't necessarily a bad thing. As in many areas of life, a long and careful process of growth can produce far healthier results than hurried strategies that attempt to rush kids from one stage of development to another.

While some family ministry advocates would disagree with or even dismiss my perspective on these two cultural dynamics, I can neither close my eyes to the facts of where kids are today *nor* be discouraged. Instead, I see the way things are as an honest and fresh starting point where Christ-centered, real discipleship can take place. I'm not discouraged, angry, or even nervous about these changes in adolescent development. If we simply acknowledge what we are dealing with and commit to loving and caring for our sons in the midst of these and other cultural realities, I believe God will produce strong men to carry the torch of faith to coming generations. But we all need help with the "baby steps" of fathering, learning how to think strategically over the long haul.

THE ESSENCE OF FATHER-SON DISCIPLESHIP

THE FATHER-SON RELATIONSHIP IS PERHAPS THE MOST IMPORTANT discipleship opportunity in the life of a young man. As a father walks with God and invites his son into that journey, the son has the best chance to experience for himself the essence of a vibrant, alive faith. To begin understanding this process, it's important to ask two fundamental questions:

- What *exactly is* a disciple?
- What is the essence of father-son discipleship?

According to the New Testament, an easy definition of "disciple" is a follower of Jesus Christ who "walks" as Jesus did: "Whoever claims to live in him must walk as Jesus did" (1 John 2:6). Another definition, similar yet a little more descriptive, is that whoever believes in Jesus Christ and expresses that faith by loving others is a disciple: "And this is his command: to believe in the name of his Son, Jesus Christ, and to love one another as he commanded us" (1 John 3:23).

Both of these definitions are examples of the consistently simple message of the Bible. A disciple is a person who has responded to God's love in Christ Jesus by believing (or equally as true to the Greek word used in 1 John 3:23, by "trusting" or "having faith") in God and his Word—in the message that proclaims freedom, peace, and restored relationship in a fractured world. A disciple is therefore someone who expresses this belief by committing to and walking in a life of unconditional, sacrificial, sometimes illogical and often unnoticed *love*. This is consistent and clear throughout the Scriptures. God calls men and women to trust him, and he then gives them the power to truly love. A disciple loves God, others, and even—made possible by the cross—himself: "The entire law is summed up in a single command: 'Love your neighbor as yourself'" (Galatians 5:14).

So, as a father, how do you *lead* and *guide* your son into this discipleship relationship and lifestyle? How do you teach your son, in word and actions, what it looks like for him to fully trust Jesus Christ and to surrender his life for others in love?

A father who seeks to disciple his son must recognize that life is different for his son than it was for him. He must be willing to rise above assumptions and stale propositions. And a father must recognize that the life he lives will become the most indelible voice his son will ever hear.

Frank, a fairly well-known and well-respected Christian leader, learned this too late. He has always been seen as a man who knows what it means to live an authentic Christian life. He's married and has two sons who as children attended church, were active in youth ministry, and went to Christian college. From all appearances, Frank and his wife were a shining example that being a Christian parent isn't that hard if you are faithful, committed, and live the way people expect you to live.

During the past decade, Frank learned the hard way that much of what he *thought* was authentic Christian living was actually living by the numbers. He confided in me the struggles he and his family had encountered the last few years. He'd thought that as long as his family had family devotionals together every week, as long as his boys were involved in church activities, and as long as public personas were maintained, all would be well. What he has discovered is that life is much more complicated and delicate than that.

According to Frank, his older son had never talked

with him about his sexual escapades because he felt he couldn't tell his dad the truth. This deceptive behavior has cost his son his marriage, for years of hidden and unfettered sexual stimulation and experience kept him from being faithful to his Christian bride. His younger son confessed that he "never was really a Christian," and he's living estranged from his family, thousands of miles away from home. The last time Frank and his younger son talked, they argued about his lifestyle, and just before his son hung up on him, he said, "You never knew me." Frank is heartbroken, but feels he has nowhere to take his pain. He told a friend that Christians would never understand what his family is going through.

Frank and I are a lot alike. I'm just a few years younger than he is. Since the day I knew I was going to be a father, I dreamed for my sons to know and love God. Neither Frank nor I want to do *anything* to get in the way of that. But Frank's story is a wake-up call to all of us. Loving my kids to Christ is a much deeper, proactive, and relationally focused process than I'd ever thought. It takes understanding my sons, it takes listening, and it takes the willingness to slog through the mud of adolescence alongside my boys.

The relationship between a father and his son, then, is perhaps the key factor in raising a son who has a heart for God and a love of people. A relationship with Christ is most effectively communicated when the messenger lives out of a vital determination to *be the message* to his son. This kind of disciple, and this definition of discipleship, is in short supply today (and, I believe, has been for a very long time). And yet even in the midst of these dynamics, an adolescent needs and almost always internally *longs for* an adult who cares.

So, leading and guiding your son on a journey with Christ takes *at least* as much commitment as the practice of spiritual disciplines and/or doctrinal precision. Perhaps more so. Nuances of theology, spiritual "consistency" (an oxymoron in the life of an adolescent), and even some of the specific "duties" of the faith—daily quiet time, active involvement in a youth group, dressing "properly" for church—have much less of an impact than an authentic, Christ-centered, life-on-life, soul-to-soul relationship between a developing not-yet-adult son and a developing, striving, and maturing father.

FRAMEWORK FOR GROWTH

This book offers three main areas for fathers to consider as they seek to influence sons for Christ—the marks of any disciple, the goals of the fatherhood discipleship process, and a father's unique role in a son's journey toward spiritual adulthood. What matters for authentic discipleship is what has always mattered to God, and it's summarized in Micah 6:6-8:

> With what shall I come before the LORD and bow down before the exalted God? Shall I come before him with burnt offerings, with calves a year old? Will the LORD be pleased with thousands of rams, with ten thousand rivers of oil? Shall I offer my firstborn for my transgression, the fruit of my body for the sin of my soul? He has showed you, O man, what is good. And what does the LORD require of you? To act justly and to love mercy and to walk humbly with your God.

Although some may scoff at such a description of discipleship, to condense the essence of faith into "to act justly and to love mercy and to walk humbly" is *not* the same as "watering down" the gospel. Yes, disciplines such as knowledge, teaching, prayer, and fasting are important aspects of historic Christian faith. But these are not the *central* markers of a life led by the Father, filled by the Holy Spirit, and mediated by Jesus Christ. A changed character is what marks a follower of the Incarnate Word. That's the key to training young disciples, and it's the message of this book.

Consider your own dreams for your son. What markers of faith are you hoping he will display? Your list might look like this: He loves the church, ministers to others, tithes, prays consistently, believes the essential doctrines of the church, and reads and even studies his Bible. These and other observable spiritual activities, interests, and commitments are tremendous. It's so encouraging to hear your son pray a breakthrough prayer or to connect faith with a decision about what kind of music to listen to. But remember, Jesus' greatest adversaries were the Pharisees, who were really into being externally "holy." You probably know people who look and talk like sincere followers of Jesus Christ but use power or position to do damage to others. While external markers are great indicators that God's working in your son, remember that God is just as interested in what is happening on the *inside* of your boy and in how that impacts other people.

This is such a crucial point as you seek to present an honest, authentic understanding of the gospel to your son. In Isaiah 1, God's passion on this point is clear:

"The multitude of your sacrifices—what are they to me?" says the LORD. "I have more than enough of burnt offerings, of rams and the fat of fattened animals; I have no pleasure in the blood of bulls and lambs and goats. When you come to appear before me, who has asked this of you, this trampling of my courts? Stop bringing meaningless offerings! Your incense is detestable to me. New Moons, Sabbaths and convocations—I cannot bear your evil assemblies. Your New Moon festivals and your appointed feasts my soul hates. They have become a burden to me; I am weary of bearing them. When you spread out your hands in prayer, I will hide my eyes from you; even if you offer many prayers, I will not listen. Your hands are full of blood; wash and make yourselves clean. Take your evil deeds out of my

sight! Stop doing wrong, learn to do right! Seek
justice, encourage the oppressed. Defend the
cause of the fatherless, plead the case of the
widow." (verses 11-17)

What matters to God is that his people would turn to
him *as God* and follow him wherever and however he leads.
And he calls those who love him to a much deeper, more
pervasive and radical attachment to him and his purposes
than what most believers refer to as "discipleship." God is
interested in the heart, and he won't stop pursuing his children until he has won their internal, authentic devotion.
Spiritual disciplines and spiritual activities *are* valuable tools
for the person who longs to know God and live in intimate
communion with him. They're the means to the end, or the
goal, of faith. But your faith relationship with your son will
focus on a much more foundational journey, looking both
toward the end product of the task of discipling another and
toward what it means to live now as one set free by Christ
in a dark, lonely, and at times hostile world.

FROM FATHER TO SON

1. Write your son a one-page letter, telling him how much
   you love him and are committed to being the most supportive dad you can be. Tell him you'll need his help, setting the stage for a two-way relationship of trust.

2. Sponsor a father-son "discussion" with some other dads
   and their sons. You contact the dads, and your son invites
   the boys (anywhere from three to five father-son pairs).
   Don't reveal the specifics of the meeting; just let the kids
   know that as dads, you want to listen to what the sons
   need from them as fathers.

3. Invite your son out to breakfast or dessert with your pastor.
   Get him to tell you and your son his story. After the experience, help your son to see that a pastor is just a person
   like every other person, but that God has given him a
   unique life calling. Try to help your son to recognize that

he is every bit as called as your pastor, and each one is unique and necessary in God's family.

GO FOR IT!

Starting right now (and throughout adolescence) make it a goal to spend *at least* half a day per month with your son, doing whatever he wants to do. Your conversations will deepen naturally over time, and you'll be building the consistent relationship you'll need to connect soul to soul. Beware: Don't promise this unless you intend to fulfill it.

FROM FATHER TO FATHER

1. Share with each other your experiences of being raised by your fathers, both joys and disappointments. How did your father's relationship with you affect your faith today?

2. What spiritual disciplines or external markers (regular prayer, Bible reading/memorization, church involvement) are beneficial for your sons' faith development right now? Which of these expectations may possibly be a point of rebellion or lack of interest? Why? How do you pick which ones to encourage and which ones to let slide, at least for now?

3. Look again at Frank's story (page 18). How do you react to this story? Have you seen anything similar? How can you try to avoid what happened with Frank's sons?

CHAPTER 2

THE MARKS OF A DISCIPLE: A LOVER

People were bringing little children to Jesus to have him touch them, but the disciples rebuked them. When Jesus saw this, he was indignant. He said to them, "Let the little children come to me, and do not hinder them, for the kingdom of God belongs to such as these. I tell you the truth, anyone who will not receive the kingdom of God like a little child will never enter it."

—MARK 10:13-15

I COMPLETED MY DOCTORAL PROGRAM IN HUMAN COMMUNICAtions Studies at the University of Denver, a relatively typical secular university not exactly known for its warm ideological embrace of traditional Christianity. During my first year, I was in a seminar studying political rhetoric with seven other Ph.D. students. This was during the fall of 1992, and in Colorado there was a heated battle over Amendment 2, which became known as the "gay rights initiative." This was a highly charged time, and our class had opportunity to be involved in some fairly significant media consultations during the fall term. To my knowledge, I was the only practicing Christian in the class.

Almost daily, I found myself defending the beliefs, attitudes, and behaviors of fellow believers to the other students. (I later learned the professor was also a believer, but during the quarter he said little either way.) We generally got on well, but one day the tensions came to a head. One of my classmates—a tender, smart, warm, engaging lesbian— entered the room crying. I'd worked hard to win her friendship. She walked straight over to me, holding a gospel tract in her hand, and said, "I just got my car badly keyed along the side, and all I found was this on the windshield." I stupidly asked her how she knew these were related, 'and she looked at me with more sadness than anger and said, "You don't know what I go through here. Ever since I put a 'No on 2' sticker on my car, I've been yelled at and threatened, had notes left on my car, and now this. Why do Christians hate me so much?"

I was speechless and ashamed. I was brokenhearted for my friend. Like all of us, she needed to see and feel the mercy and tenderness of God, but what she experienced instead was the scorn of his people. I like to think that our relationship made some sort of difference in her perception, but she was already considerably wounded by "us." I hope I was an exception to her rule.

HE WAS INDIGNANT

I'VE OFTEN WONDERED WHAT THE LORD FELT ABOUT ALL OF THIS. Jesus made it very clear that the bottom line of the gospel is to "love your neighbor as yourself." In response to the question, "Who is my neighbor?" Jesus used the parable of the good Samaritan (see Luke 10:25-37) to say that if I see someone in pain or in need, that person is the neighbor I'm called to comfort, care for, and love.

The phrase "He was indignant . . ." from the passage at the beginning of this chapter is a window into the heart of God toward not only "his" children, but *all* children! This passage makes clear that God is crazy about kids. We rarely use the word "indignant" today. In English, it describes an anger fueled by a violation of something that is dignified or of great worth or value. In Greek, the idea is also related to grief and even frustration. Jesus was *indignant* that the disciples were interrupting the chaos of children mobbing him. He was grieved, angry, and clearly frustrated that they didn't understand who he was, what mattered to him, or the authentic essence of the kingdom. This event prompted Jesus to launch into one of his more pointed lessons: "Anyone who will not receive the kingdom of God like a little child will never enter it."

There's something fresh, clean, and pure about most little children. They haven't yet built up the capacity for effective manipulation, nor have they been so jaded by the realities of life that they screen their passions. Children are free to pursue their passions with radical, unfiltered abandonment. They're free to run and jump into the arms of those they long to touch. They're free to love. This is also the first and primary mark of a disciple; therefore, it's the ultimate goal in discipling your son.

WHAT ARE WE KNOWN FOR?

WHAT'S THE FIRST THING THAT CROSSES THE MIND OF THE AVERAGE person on the street when asked about his perception of Christians? Recently, I asked some students to do on-the-street interviews to get a firsthand answer to this question. The negative reactions the students experienced, and the anger lurking just below the surface, threw them off considerably. People weren't *mean,* but they were clearly not without strong opinions either. The one common attitude that consistently emerged? We're seen as narrow-minded, political bigots who refuse to respect other people's right to disagree with us. Most believe that Christians violate one of our culture's most preciously held values: freedom to think on one's own.

I don't want to engage the merits of such a description here. But because it's such a common perception, it *does* point to a central problem we have as a band of people committed to walking together to honor our God. There's a huge disconnect between what people think of us and what we're called to be about. These next few chapters offer four "marks of a disciple." The first is that a disciple is a lover. *That* is the primary distinctive mark of someone who trusts and follows Jesus Christ.

WHAT IS A "LOVER"?

WHAT DOES IT MEAN TO LOVE OTHERS AS FOLLOWERS OF CHRIST? How far does our commitment to love others go? Do we ever take a stand? Should we ever retreat from the truth or compromise? Or, maybe love is simply some method-based formula that keeps everybody happy and feeling good.

A cursory look at the life of Jesus—the quintessential Lover—makes clear that his goal was not to make everyone happy. Some people hated Jesus and many others distrusted him. He didn't play games and he didn't pull punches. But with every individual and in each situation, even those where he was tough or angry (the turning over the tables in John 2, for instance), Jesus Christ *loved!*

What, then, does this mark of a disciple look like in a son?

A lover-son is someone who has made a decision to walk with God in such a profound way that he allows the Holy Spirit to love others through him. He sees others through Jesus' eyes, not as the world (or even other believers) sees them. He doesn't look at what others can do for him or can provide him, but rather values each individual as God's precious creation worth dying for. He continually looks for opportunities to be a force of healing and reconciliation. He's someone who knows that Paul was right when he proclaimed, "The entire law is summed up in a single command: 'Love your neighbor as yourself'" (Galatians 5:14).

Close friends saw a subtle yet profound glimmer of this when their son was in junior high school, but because it wasn't on their discipleship radar, they almost missed it. Josh was a rather wild, active seventh-grader who tolerated the youth group but hated church. He was far more interested in friends, sports, and girls than in anything smacking of spirituality. His parents were very worried about his faith.

But one brief announcement in Sunday school gave them a window into what God was doing on the inside of their son.

An inner-city tutoring ministry needed volunteers to teach under-served elementary children how to read and study. The announcement went out to high school and adult ministries all over Denver, but because their church had combined junior and senior high kids that Sunday, Josh heard the pitch. He came home and announced that he was "going to teach kids in the city." Right there he had committed himself to dropping his basketball team to work with one kid every Monday night all year.

His parents tried to dissuade him with every argument they could think of, but he had an answer for everything— there's next year's basketball team; he could get a ride with an adult couple who lived near them; and he would always have his homework done before he left. When the organizers found out he was in junior high, and they called to tell him he couldn't do it, he simply said, "Why not? Huh? Why *not?* I can read!" All the adult arguments lost out, and Josh spent a year loving a third-grader in the name of Christ. They prayed together every week, they talked on the phone, and Josh even helped lead the Young Life club with the other tutors (all adults—no high school kids signed up). He was still Josh—a wild, fun, uninterested-in-church seventh-grader. But he was now Josh, lover of someone else for Jesus' sake.

Your son has the capacity to express his love for Jesus Christ no matter how old he is. What matters is how you frame faith for him. He needs to be taught that God first calls him to be a lover-disciple. To more fully appreciate this idea, it may be helpful to note what being a lover does not look like.

WHAT A LOVER-DISCIPLE DOES NOT LOOK LIKE

SOMEONE WHO BLINDLY EMBRACES ALL BEHAVIOR AS HEALTHY OR acceptable. Some people withhold love because they're afraid the recipient might misinterpret it as acquiescence to certain behaviors or lifestyle choices. The logic is that if we "get involved" with people we disagree with, we'll be seen as compromising. Most adults know better, and we even have an axiom to describe this: "Love the sinner; hate the sin." But the walls around our Christian cultural city have become thicker over the years. We've become adept at building attitudes and a value system that *separate* us from others to the point where our only option for loving is from a distance. Thus we rejoice over missionaries who work day by day with poor, broken children in India, yet gasp and flee when tattooed skateboarders burst into our youth programs. We have become so nervous, so con- flicted, and so entrenched that the call to love is often our last consideration, to the point where we ultimately cease to even care much about those "outside."

Yet the Scriptures seem to scream at us in response to our callous "indifference and retreat" mentality. Because Jesus was indignant at the disciples for "hindering" the chil- dren, wouldn't he be equally indignant when we forget how to love? This is the primary call of the gospel; a lover- disciple, constantly provoked by the Spirit, realizes this. A lover is concerned for truth, integrity, and holiness as well as kindness and compassion. A son who is a lover-disciple will want to find tangible ways to love those who don't or won't share his perspective.

A friend of mine was concerned that his son was being swept into negative and destructive attitudes toward a par- ticular ethnic group. This dad decided to invite his teenage son to volunteer with him as a tee-ball coach for a summer with these kids. Without the dad having to say a word about his motives, his son fell in love with these children and their families over the course of the season. The dad simply reminded his son what a great privilege it is to serve God by getting to know his people. Over the summer, his son learned to be a lover.

A person without moral or ethical conviction. In the world at large, morality has sunk to an all-time low. In Christian academic circles, the discipline of ethics reminds

Christians that our faith compels us to be concerned with justice, peace, overcoming destructive powers, and displaying indiscriminate mercy. But in the everyday Christian world, we seem to have landed on a morality that has little or nothing to do with *people*. This misrepresents God's view of morality. Ethics is about people and how we live together. A lover-disciple realizes this.

Take the teaching of sexual ethics to our sons. One way to focus on our sons' spiritual growth would be to draw bold, clear boundaries of behavior (such as "no R-rated movies") without ever really talking to them about the reasons behind these rules. Instead, perhaps we should be in a constant teaching mode, looking for those few but precious teachable moments when we can point out God's loving heart regarding our sexuality. God isn't against sex, but is angered by the way we use our sexual drives and urges to hurt or devalue—in our actions or our minds—other people. All lust and sexual rebellion is more about hurting others than simply crossing an arbitrary line.

Someone who is committed to a "live and let live" philosophy of life. A lover-disciple doesn't wait for others to come to him. Your son is called to be a disciple who has responded to what Henri Nouwen calls the "First Love," the love God has for us to experience in relationship to himself. This God-initiated First Love can't stand in the background of life and simply prompt your boy's growth and faith so as to allow him to sit back and bask in the warmth of God's mercy, forgiveness, and love. This kind of love, by its very nature, *compels* your son to action. As he grows in his relationship with God, he will become increasingly aware that the Holy Spirit is constantly calling him to be on the move with love. Your son, as a follower of Jesus Christ, is called to a proactive, focused, single-minded commitment to loving others in God's name. What an honor. What a responsibility!

I've been in youth ministry for almost thirty years, and one of the most significant lessons I've learned is that authentic faith is always accompanied by a pursuing, loving spirit. Where God is, love is *always* the driving force. Shawn, a young man who never knew his father, turned his life over to Christ during his freshman year of high school. That year he was obnoxious, arrogant, and abusive. Out of his pain of being abandoned by his dad, he'd internally decided to take it out on the world. But as Shawn grew in his trust in Christ, as he allowed God to be his "father to the fatherless," his heart was visibly softened. Shawn is now in his mid-thirties, and he is one of the most generous, tender, and committed lovers of people I've ever known. He's also a *great* father to his three kids.

WHAT A LOVER-DISCIPLE DOES LOOK LIKE

SOMEONE WHO VALUES THE DIGNITY OF EACH INDIVIDUAL. TO A lover-son, every person is a rich depository of God's image. Jesus' use of the story of the good Samaritan reminds us to love those outside the ring of natural relationship. This example expresses God's heart toward each individual. The parables of the lost (the stories of the lost sheep, the lost coin, and the lost son in Luke 15) *all* portray the passionate and focused love God has for each unique individual. It may be incredible to ponder, but true nonetheless: there's not a soul alive whom God has not personally and intricately designed with great care and intense energy. And, because God is love, each one of these "little ones" is deeply and profoundly cherished.

My friend Kurt is a pastor. Because his own childhood consisted of a legalistic understanding of faith, as his own sons were growing up he held fast to the notion that they needed to come to faith slowly and relationally rather than through rules and regulations. When the boys were young, they'd sometimes wear T-shirts and ripped jeans to church. But Kurt defended his boys. He and his wife were far more concerned that their sons come to see faith summarized in loving others, rather than how "Christian" they look. Kurt took them to the inner city to serve the poor, and he and his wife included them in their decisions on giving. Their sons, both in their twenties now, are in full-time ministry.

Kurt's sons were trained in the essence of the gospel, to be lover-disciples. A lover-disciple ultimately has one calling and therefore one vocation: to see every person as God sees him, and to love every person as God loves him.

Someone who recognizes that all of us are fragile, broken people. An occupational hazard of those who are actively involved in some form of Christian service or leadership is that we can easily believe we're somehow immune from the frailties of this world. This is not only highly dangerous; it's also flat wrong. Whether he's a pastor, a writer (me), or a committed dad, a discipler needs to make the important confession that "there, but for the grace of God, go I." You know how fragile you are and how delicate a dance it is to maintain a life of faith that has integrity. As hard as it is to admit, those who do awful things are not all that different from me. Lover-disciples not only know this, but also keep this realization at the forefront of their lives.

Tom, my pastor several years ago, has been a real hero for me in this area. He often talked about his rather sordid background and how Jesus Christ pulled him from a life of brokenness, arrogance, and pride into the kingdom. As a husband, father, and friend, Tom is remarkably consistent in how he critiques others, even those who have clearly failed and hurt others on the way down. When a mutual friend of ours made some choices that broke up two marriages, Tom wept. He was *indignant,* yet he was compassionate in his concern even for the friend who'd been selfish. I'm so grateful that my boys know Tom and have experienced his grace up close and personal.

Someone who walks in love more than he talks about love. Let's face it; many people don't care for Christians or the church. It's possible that most really don't dislike Christians as much as they don't understand Christians. Wherever their misunderstandings come from, some people think that even though we may talk a lot about love, collectively we're not very good at it.

The point is that we're not called to try to change the

world's *perception* of us as followers of Jesus Christ. Instead, we're called to be salt and light in a world longing for love. It's good and right to describe the essence of our faith as a call to love. But it's even more important, and far more powerful, to actually love.

I'm hopeful because most of the Christian fathers I know are very committed to developing sons who love God and therefore love people. This is your call, Dad: to unfalteringly maintain your focus on this great goal of your son's faith. You're building a disciple whose first and central priority of faith is to love his neighbor as himself.

FROM FATHER TO SON

1. Look together for an example of someone showing extraordinary love and compassion for another, either in his life, your life, or the world. Discuss how God felt about this. Gently lead your son to see that this is God's major concern for his people.

2. Scheme with your son to do something unexpected for the women in your home. Connect this to your love for them as followers of Christ.

3. When you hear someone being harshly critical of another person, discuss with your son how this makes him feel. Let him see how we regularly need forgiveness and compassion when we make mistakes. Discuss how we can learn how to walk in this tension before God.

4. Write your son an e-mail letting him know where you've seen him be a lover-disciple.

GO FOR IT!

Volunteer together for something that serves those who have a need, whether it's tutoring, working alongside people (Habitat for Humanity, for example), or helping out in a sports program. The activity doesn't really matter, as long as your son somehow connects that you're doing this for others in response to God's love for you both.

FROM FATHER TO FATHER

1. Discuss what it means to live like a little child (see Mark 10:13-16), especially in terms of how we live as lover-disciples.

2. What are your raw reactions to this chapter and to the idea that the primary call of the Christian is to love? In what ways do you struggle with this?

3. What's one area/group/issue where it's hard for you to be lover-disciples? How has this affected your ability to lead your sons?

CHAPTER 3

THE MARKS OF A DISCIPLE:
A RELATER

> Be kind and compassionate to one another, forgiving each other, just as in Christ God forgave you. Be imitators of God, therefore, as dearly loved children and live a life of love, just as Christ loved us and gave himself up for us as a fragrant offering and sacrifice to God.
>
> —EPHESIANS 4:32–5:2

WHEN I WAS GROWING UP, MY FATHER WAS LIKE MOST DADS I knew—a good guy, hardworking, and busy. He loved me, but because of his job and life, it was hard for him to be deeply involved in the activities that took up my time. But one day he showed up and convinced me of the value and power of having a fan.

Although I am not exactly an Olympic athlete, I grew up playing most every sport and doing fairly well. During my sophomore year in high school, I happened to be the starting free safety on a championship-caliber junior varsity football team. Going into the final game of the season, we were undefeated and playing our cross-town rival—also undefeated. As I prepared to leave that Saturday morning, I asked my dad if he could come to the game. I told him how great a game it would be, and that the winner would be league champion. I subtly tried to sell him on the competitive merits of the contest. He obviously knew how much I wanted him there, so he told me he would try to come.

During the game, I glanced up once or twice to see if he'd shown up. But it was a big game (for both our team and the varsity team) so the crowd was huge and I never found him. The game went back and forth until in the final minute—more by luck than by skill—I made the play of my life that caused an interception and sealed the win for our team. As my teammate was running the ball down the field, with twenty panting tenth-graders chasing him, one little defensive back (me) was just getting up from the hit that forced the interception. As the crowd was yelling, focused on the far end of the field, and as I tried to clear my head to get back into the play, I heard one voice rise above the roar of the crowd: "Way to go, Chappie!"

And then I saw him—standing at the top of the stands above the student section, a middle-aged guy in a business suit screaming, jumping up and down, waving his arms at me. My father had been there—to see *me!* My dad had come to my game.

Years later it dawned on me what a gift that was to me. I'd tried to get my dad to the game based on the competition. But he came for one reason: to be the fan of one, his son. He was there to support me, encourage me, and experience something in my life with me. He didn't really care how other players did or even what the final outcome would be. He was indeed a fan, but not of our junior varsity team. He was *my* fan. He was there for me! And in the deepest part of who I am, that is exactly what I needed and even longed for—I so desperately wanted a fan.

I don't think most people would describe my father as a "relater," especially in the way he raised his sons. Few men of his era saw their role as being relational co-nurturers with their wives in dealing with the kids—even the boys. The way he and my mom worked out their roles was more or less along the traditional lines of the day and, unfortunately, this included an unspoken decree that relegated my father to being the provider and protector of our family. It was my mother's job to nurture us. It was my father's to earn the money for us to live. Yet this vivid memory of my game is but one example of the many, many times he *was* a powerfully relational, nurturing voice in my life. When I push aside my definitions of "nurture," I realize that my dad was and continues to be an anchor of support in my life. We just don't talk about him and his role in those terms. But I will nonetheless always be grateful for the subtle ways he taught me that relationships and caring matter.

Some dads may place different emphases or attach different words to how they nourish and encourage their sons as well as lead them into manhood. You may feel comfortable describing what it means to be a man of God by pointing to a powerful military leader like William Wallace (of *Braveheart* fame). Or, you may look to one of the most courageous people of the twentieth century, Mother Teresa, to give your son an image or model to shoot for. Whatever example you follow, you undoubtedly want to be a nurturing, caring, supportive influence in the life of your son *and* you want to teach him to be the same to others. We all want to be the kind of father who lets his son know that he matters, that he's cherished and valued, no matter what position or instrument he plays, what other kids say about him, or how well he does in school. God has called us to be every bit as nurturing with our children as mothers are. It just looks different for dads, and from dad to dad.

Here's what I see at Friday night football games in our little community: When one of the players makes a great play, the parents all look over and yell to that player's parents—usually the dad. I feel it myself—great pride and satisfaction when my son makes a play or even sustains a decent block. "Did you see Rob? He made that a gain by staying with that linebacker!" Yes, it's fun when our team wins. But like every other dad, I watch my son on the sidelines when he's not playing at least as much as I watch the game. I wonder what he's thinking and how he's feeling. I want him to know that *he* is what matters to me and that I am and will always be his biggest fan. I also want him to treat his teammates and opponents with respect, to see the game as a game, and to be kind and supportive of the other players even when he's treated unfairly. I want to be his fan, and I want him to learn how to be the fan of others.

I think nearly every father, when he thinks about it, intuitively recognizes this. Life is *not* really about perform-ance. It's much more about connection and caring. We may say we want our son to be some kind of a "strong warrior" and a driving force in the world, but in our hearts—at least for guys that understand God's kingdom and follow Christ—we're really more concerned with how he treats people, how he cares for others, and that he is just, honest, and kind.

GOD'S DESIGN FOR MEN – RELATER-DISCIPLES

So God created man in his own image, in the image of God he created him; male and female he created them; . . . God saw all that he had made, and it was very good. (Genesis 1:27,31)

THIS IS HOW THE BOOK OF GENESIS DESCRIBES THE CREATION OF humanity. We all—male and female—are created in the image of God. And although there are many who claim that women are more "naturally" prone to relationships and intimacy than men, that image is primarily *relational,* for *all* of God's people. Every man, then, is designed by God to live, work, and exist within the context of relation-ships. Yes, there are some unique expressions of strength that may also be part of the package in this image for men, for God is a God of power ("For God did not give us a spirit of timidity, but a spirit of power." 2 Timothy 1:7), but this power is accessible by all of his children, not just men. Women, in our culture anyway, are said to be more nur-turing and relationally focused "gatherers" than men. We men, on the other hand, are often described as more aggressive "hunters" who are less able and even willing to sustain deep and intimate relationships with others. These tendencies are true for many of us in our society. But we should not allow ourselves to stay stuck in that stereotype. We need to go to the Bible to recalibrate our understanding of what it means to be a man, especially a man of God. We need to get back to the basics of God's intent for us as men so we can help our sons to grow into the kind of men that honor the Lord and are useful in his kingdom.

The Bible, however, seems to be relatively silent on what it really means to *be* a man. Yes, Scripture contains some discussion of the relationship between men and women in marriage and offers limited recommendations for gender role definitions in the early church, but it's virtually silent on any other distinctions between men and women. In fact, it's difficult to conclude that the Bible authoritatively claims that men and women are all that different. God's Word is far more interested in the places we're alike than where we are different. Of course, there are differences between men and women, but when it comes to living as disciples, we men have very little gender-driven wiggle room. We're called to the same sort of character and relationships as women disciples. That means that you *and* your son, whatever image of manhood you land on, are called ultimately to be relater-disciples.

Fortunately, the Bible is helpful and consistent in showing us how to be disciples of Jesus Christ. The irony is that many of the biblical qualities of relater-disciples are attributed to women in today's culture, even though they're actually important characteristics for both men and women.

Take a look at the following list describing the qualities a lover of God is called to have.

- Gentle: "Let your gentleness be evident to all. The Lord is near" (Philippians 4:5).
- Merciful: "Be merciful, just as your Father is merciful" (Luke 6:36).
- Tender: "If you have any encouragement from being united with Christ, if any comfort from his love, if

any fellowship with the Spirit, if any tenderness and compassion" (Philippians 2:1).

- Kind: "Love is patient, love is kind" (1 Corinthians 13:4).
- Clear in communicating: "My dear brothers, take note of this: Everyone should be quick to listen, slow to speak and slow to become angry" (James 1:19). "Therefore each of you must put off false-hood and speak truthfully to his neighbor, for we are all members of one body" (Ephesians 4:25).
- Nurturing: "As apostles of Christ we could have been a burden to you, but we were gentle among you, like a mother caring for her little children. We loved you so much that we were delighted to share with you not only the gospel of God but our lives as well, because you had become so dear to us" (1 Thessalonians 2:6-8).
- Comforting: "Praise be to the God and Father of our Lord Jesus Christ, the Father of compassion and the God of all comfort, who comforts us in all our troubles, so that we can comfort those in any trou-ble with the comfort we ourselves have received from God" (2 Corinthians 1:3-4).
- Affectionate: "Love one another with mutual affec-tion" (Romans 12:10, NRSV).
- Hospitable: "Share with God's people who are in need. Practice hospitality" (Romans 12:13).

DAVID, THE RELATER-DISCIPLE

MANY PEOPLE THINK OF KING DAVID, THE GREATEST KING IN Israel's history, as the prototypical man's man. Over the course of his life he was a powerful military ruler, a pas-sionate political leader, and even a skilled manipulator of people and circumstances when it suited his needs: "Whenever David attacked an area, he did not leave a man or woman alive, but took sheep and cattle, donkeys and camels, and clothes" (1 Samuel 27:9). He was a strong, intense, and externally fearless leader.

However, although he was a man committed to God, he was also a first-rate sinner. David even went to the point of murdering a man to steal his beautiful wife (Bathsheba). Still, the Bible makes him out to be one of the most significant spiritual leaders in the history of Israel. He's even described as a man "after [God's] own heart" (Acts 13:22). Though he was brutal, even savage, as a military leader, and was an adulterer who conspired to murder, he was also a direct ancestor of Jesus (who was called "Son of David"). How do we put all this together?

The answer lies in David's heart, in his authentic willingness to be God's man, even when he failed. David's life and journey present a paradox for modern Christians—in so many ways he was a shining example of how we should *not* live. Yet God saw in David a spark of passionate faith and commitment that pleased him. How David responded to God's anger in his darkest days eventually caused God to restore him to the point where the Bible describes him as nearly sinless: "You have not been like my servant David, who kept my commands and followed me with all his heart, doing only what was right in my eyes" (1 Kings 14:8). For all his faults, David sincerely loved God and was driven by his desire to serve him.

David was a great example of what it means to be a man of God. It's *not* his ability or power as a military or political leader, however, that makes him such a model of faith. It's the deeper essence of the man himself. Throughout the Scriptures we see two clear ways that his soft, relational heart was an even more prominent feature of his life than his ability as a warrior. First, David was the principle writer of many of the psalms. These words show us David's humble and authentic heart before the Lord.

Second, David saw life relationally, which we notice especially in the biblical description of his friendship with Jonathan. Soon after David entered the national scene by leading the charge against Goliath and the Philistines, he committed himself to an extremely intense friendship with the king's son, Jonathan. From the beginning of their relationship, David and Jonathan were "one in spirit" (1 Samuel 18:1), and "Jonathan made a covenant with David because he loved him as himself" (1 Samuel 18:3). This relationship was a major factor in David's ascent to the throne, yet it was far more than that. To both men, this relationship was more important than any career aspirations.

This is an example of what it means to follow Christ. David and Jonathan's relationship is not just an interesting sidebar to David's life story. It is core. David knew that his life belonged to God and that having close friendships was more important than anything else. To be a disciple means to see life as an adventure of faith experienced in relationships and lived out of community. Nothing else matters in God's scheme of things than to trust, know, and follow Jesus Christ and to love others as we love ourselves. This is what it means to be a relater-disciple.

LIFE THROUGH THE FILTER OF RELATIONSHIPS

HOW DO YOU CONVINCE YOUR SON THAT THIS IS ALL THERE IS TO life? In a world where he's bombarded with the message that competition and conquest, performance and winning are all that matter, how do you turn this around for him? How do you build into him a commitment to living as a relater-disciple? The first step may be obvious, but it's easier said than done: You must be convinced of this yourself. Only then will he begin to see firsthand that this is how God intended for him to live. Teaching him to be a relater-disciple is far more about modeling and creating an environment where he experiences life as relationship than it is about "doing" discipleship activities. It's a mindset that starts with you.

That said, keep in mind what internally you already know—that a relater-disciple is a man who sees all of life through the filter of relationships. He understands that God created men, just like women, in his image. Therefore men are created for relationships. Tasks, work, responsibilities, ambition, and even faith are held in balance by a central commitment to the integrity and sanctity of relationships — to God, to others, and to yourself.

Relationship with God

The relater-disciple learns that the Christian faith begins with a personal, intimate relationship between the individual believer and God, and this love relationship produces the kind of person that cares about others. For your son to grow in his faith, he needs to realize that his response to God's love for him is the starting point for all of life, and this will flow into all other relationships. Nothing else really matters. Jesus consistently affirmed that this relationship is central and that the intimacy and reality of this fundamental connection affects all other relationships. Doing tasks, fulfilling commitments, and even performing sacred duties (like spiritual disciplines or acts of Christian service) must all be understood as both *expressions* of the relationship between a believer and God and a *means* to deepen that relationship. These two angles of what are sometimes called the "practices" of faith comprise the practical expression of the Christian life.

A few years ago, I was speaking at a youth conference and I received an anonymous note from a counselor. He was forty-one years old and the father of a boy on the trip. He'd listened to me the previous night talk about how God was our biggest fan ("If God is for us, who can be against us?" Romans 8:31), he likes us, and he came to have a relationship with us. His note tells how he experienced my message:

> I can't explain how I feel right now. I've been a
> Christian my whole life but not a very good one.
> I've always thought that being a Christian meant I
> did the right things, and I never felt like I was
> very good at it. After last night I'm both angry
> and glad. I'm angry that no one told me this

sooner. And I'm *really* angry that I've passed on
what I thought to my son. But as we talked last
night, it's so great to know that God is interested
in *me*. My son and I are now on that journey you
talked about last night, together. Thanks.

That man understands what it means to be a relater-disciple.

What are you teaching your son about the essence of
faith? Does he see all of life as a loving response to what
God has done, or is it a "duty dance" with a God who is
distant and disgusted with us? In the famous "fruit of the
Spirit" passage in Galatians 5, fruit is a by-product of a
healthy fruit tree: "So I say, live by the Spirit, and you will
not gratify the desires of the sinful nature. . . . But the fruit
of the Spirit is love, joy, peace, patience, kindness, goodness, faithfulness, gentleness and self-control" (Galatians
5:16,22).

Notice that all of these are either directly or indirectly
relational. When someone keeps "in step with the Spirit"
(Galatians 5:25), then he'll be patient, kind, and gentle.
God doesn't want your son (or any of his children) to try
to produce fruit; he wants him to live in relationship to
himself. God will produce the fruit, and it will always be
fruit that influences other people for the better. That's what
it means to love God as a relater-disciple.

Relationship with Others

When your son connects intimately to Jesus Christ, that
relationship will always—if it is real—result in a heart that
connects with and loves others. Notice the progression of
logic that the apostle Paul uses in Philippians 2:1-5:

> If you have any encouragement from being
> united with Christ, if any comfort from his love, if
> any fellowship with the Spirit, if any tenderness
> and compassion, then make my joy complete by
> being like-minded, having the same love, being
> one in spirit and purpose. Do nothing out of

selfish ambition or vain conceit, but in humility consider others better than yourselves. Each of you should look not only to your own interests, but also to the interests of others. Your attitude should be the same as that of Christ Jesus.

Encouragement from being united with Christ. A by-product of being connected to Christ is a personal, internal sense of confidence that who I am matters. Paul reminds us that when we're in relationship with God, there are innate, sometimes unseen and unknown benefits that keep us going. If your son is experiencing an authentic, inside-out faith, he will be encouraged. Conversely, if your son's faith holds any trace of discouragement, know that it doesn't come from God. Another source is polluting the message.

Comfort from his love. As the intimacy of relationship with Jesus Christ grows, we're not only encouraged by an external relationship of being united with him; we also experience a deeper sense of security and peace. A friend of mine who read that last sentence said, "I think many men are loath to accept this benefit. We think we need to do things on our own and not burden Jesus with our petty insecurities." I agree, and as a father who is committed to leading my son into a rich, deep, authentic relationship with the "God of all comfort" (2 Corinthians 1:3), I know I have to learn how to move on from this practical threat to faith.

Fellowship with his Spirit. The Greek word used for "fellowship" here is *koinonia*—the New Testament word used to designate the most intimate union someone can have with another. This is how Paul described his longing to be identified in relationship to Jesus: "I want to know Christ and the power of his resurrection and the fellowship *[koinonia]* of sharing in his sufferings, becoming like him in his death, and so, somehow, to attain to the resurrection from the dead" (Philippians 3:10-11).

This fellowship is where you know in your gut that God is real and that he accepts you as his child. Your son's faith will ultimately rise or fall on this point: does he see his faith as God accepting him, or as him accepting God? Unless he truly believes, even knows, that God has chosen him to love and that all of life flows out of the security and confidence of that truth, nothing else will ever matter. He can pray, go to church, read the Bible, and serve the poor. But unless he knows that fellowship with God's Spirit, he'll never be free to live as a disciple.

Any tenderness and compassion. Notice how Paul, after reminding us of our status as God's friends, turns the tables. In this one simple phrase he points out that your son will be a man who is tender and compassionate *as he intimately knows God.* Do you see why you don't have to spend too much time on trying to drum up tenderness, kindness, and compassion in your son? That's God's job. It's our job to model and to create the environment where he can see that God works that way. Yes, talk about the application of this, point out where he (or even you) is *not* kind or loving, but *always* couch this in the reality of what God's Spirit is wanting to do inside of him.

Make my joy complete. The apostle is reminding us to live and respond out of the truth we know. As the discipler of your son, you can encourage him to take proactive steps to live out what God is doing on the inside.

Relationship with Self

Men today have a hard time remembering that the only thing that matters in life is relationships. Life isn't about money, security, or success. It's about love, friendship, and faithfulness. Often, the pressures of career, finances, and even marriage tend to overshadow our ability to remember that life only matters as it's filtered through relationships. As one friend put it: "Dads of kids in their teen years are often themselves going through some pretty heavy stuff. The question is, Can I use these doubts and uncertainties to soften me both to God and to my sons?"

If you identify with this, if you wonder if you have the faith or the energy to be a good model for your son, you're not alone. You know this, but you probably need to hear it over and over again: God will never give up on you or your son. He is the Great Pursuer, the Consistent Encourager. He continually whispers in your ear, "Come to me, Dad! Relax, and know that *I* am God—not you. Trust me, rest in me, and spend time getting to know me and learning to recognize my voice above the din of the world. I'll teach you and create in you a heart of love and compassion I can use."

To consistently reinforce that message to your son, you need to see him as the proverbial "poster child" of undeserved grace and unearned favor. God will never stop speaking to him, but he's chosen and appointed you to bless your son with God's words and call. Just like you, your son will become adept at self-loathing and self-doubt, especially when he's inconsistent in faith and life. But don't let that stop either of you. Look at David—a wild man, an arrogant murderer, often an emotional mess (just read the Psalms!)—yet a man after God's own heart. You and your son are called to be men who know you're loved and chosen by God, who allow that truth to convince you that you are lovable, and who therefore see all of life through the filter of relationships. You were made to be relater-disciples.

FROM FATHER TO SON

1. Take your son aside and ask him to give himself a grade on how he treats each member of your family (except you; let that flow naturally). After he has answered, share your observations. Share with him what your relationships were like in your family when you were growing up.

2. Take your son to work for half a day. At lunch, ask him to talk with you about the ways he saw you treating other people. Were you engaged in their lives? Did you care for them or just work with them? Discuss with him what it means for you to be a relater-disciple.

3. Pray with your son that two to four really close Christian brothers will come into his life and walk with him in close relationship. They may not develop into lifelong friends,

but help him to learn how to take guy relationships to a deeper level. Share with him your struggles with building those kinds of friendships with guys.

4. Write your son an e-mail telling him how you're feeling at a given moment. Find a time to discuss your thoughts and feelings at that moment, and pray together for your situation.

GO FOR IT!

Create a yearly gathering of three to five father-son pairs you trust and love. They may be from different parts of the country (or world), but commit to walking through life together by meeting regularly each year. When you meet, treat your sons as peers on the journey together. Show them how to be men in intimate long-term relationships with other men.

FROM FATHER TO FATHER

1. Start with where you are: Do you experience your relationship with God as described in this chapter? If not, what are the stumbling blocks? If so, how do you sustain that intimacy in your relationship?

2. To train your sons to be relater-disciples, you obviously need to relate to them. Discuss the things you're doing to build relational intimacy with your sons right now. Evaluate for each other to be *sure* that what you're doing — maybe coaching, going to games, helping him with homework — is really what it takes to build the kind of relationship where relational discipleship can take place. Where are the holes in your relationship?

3. What areas of your lives get in the way of you modeling life as relater-disciples? Be as honest as you can with each other, and pray for healing and growth as men committed to living the truth as well as passing it on to your sons.

CHAPTER 4

THE MARKS OF A DISCIPLE:
A TRUSTER

Lord, I already know the best way to alter my lifestyle to the best advantage for all—live like Jesus. The Christian existence ideally is to imitate what you do. You send the sun and rain on everyone, you want me to get back to the basic facts of life, to love without reservation, to distinguish between life's needs and life itself, and seek first your kingdom knowing you will meet all my other needs.

—THOMAS G. PETTEPIECE

MAYBE YOU'VE SEEN THE COMMERCIAL. AT FIRST IT FLASHED RIGHT by me, but then it caught my attention. It contained one word: "Believe." That's it—several random, wild shots of a guy playing basketball, a woman running, and others sweating, and the word "Believe." A major athletic shoe company revised its entire advertising campaign to rest on this single word. Apparently, if you believe, you'll buy the shoes.

This seems odd to me, because until September 11, 2001, this word has held little meaning for most Americans. For a season after the terrorist attacks of that morning, people experienced a heightened generic spirituality expressed in a collective crying out to God. While few labeled that national mourning as "believing," it was evident during those few weeks that we all longed for a God who would comfort us. But there was little discussion over the content of that cry—the *object* of belief was what mattered, while the *nature* of the belief was not yet on the radar.

It didn't take long for our fundamental diversity to call us back to a kind of religious truce in our national dialogue. Those of faith continued to pursue God, and everyone else tried to move on with their lives. They generally left a true belief in God somewhere in the house, but moved it back onto the shelf for times of need.

But is that *really* belief?

The interesting thing about the word "believe" is that it varies in meaning from mere intellectual assent ("I *believe* in my head"), to an emotional faith in something or someone ("I *believe* that God is there for me"), to radical, abandoned trust ("I *believe* in God and I am his"). For most people, to believe something means to think it's true. But when we're asked to believe *in* something, that tends to raise the personal bar of commitment. That's when we begin to alter our sentiment into a faith or even a trust in the object of our belief.

The kind of belief the Bible offers is much more than simply a head-faith, and it even goes beyond a "feeling" type of belief. "Believe" in the Bible is about trust, or more specifically, trusting *in* the objective of our belief. A disciple, then, is really a truster-disciple.

WHAT DOES IT MEAN TO TRUST?

WHILE MUCH OF THE RHETORIC SURROUNDING THOSE WHO WALK with Christ centers on the word "belief" or "believer," the words "believe," "faith," and "trust" found in English translations almost always come from a single Greek word, *pisteuo* (pronounced, pis-tew-o). This word summarizes the deepest, most profound idea of committed loyalty found in ancient Greek. When we read, for example, John 3:16—"For God so loved the world that he gave his one and only Son, that whoever believes in him shall not perish but have eternal life"— we're not being called to an intellectual assent to the truth of the idea that God died. This passage—and most of the other places in the New Testament that use "believe," "trust," or "faith"—calls us to a fully chosen and recognized lifelong commitment to placing our lives in God's hands.

There's nothing gray about the Scriptures' concept of belief or trust. I either trust fully in Jesus Christ as best as I understand and am capable of, or I do not. This is the mark of a disciple: one who *trusts* in Jesus Christ in a way that eliminates all natural and *super*-natural (or "spiritual") competitors. Another way to understand this is to acknowledge that the antithesis of trust is *not trusting*. In other words, those who trust Christ do their best to live on a journey where all thoughts, words, and behaviors reflect that trust. Any behaviors that do *not* reflect that trusting relationship of loyalty and commitment are therefore in opposition to God. The idea of sin, then, can be summarized as a lack of willingness (or perceived ability) to trust Jesus Christ.

You may use the word "trust" a lot in your house. As a dad, you want to know that you can trust your son. Interestingly, those who study adolescent development tell us it's vital that our sons trust *us,* especially us fathers, while they're going through the process of becoming independent people. Your son needs to trust that you'll stand firm in your commitment to love, support, and encourage him in his growth into manhood. At the same time, you want to trust that he won't make stupid or dangerous decisions along the way. Of course, it's easy for these two different types of trust to collide. You both need to remember that trust is always a two-way thing that demands incredible amounts of time and grace. Trust takes hours (and years) to develop; yet it can be severely damaged in a few short minutes. But this question is at the heart of every relationship: Can I, and will I, trust you? This is also true when it comes to faith. Do you really trust Jesus Christ?

THE PROBLEM OF SIN: LACK OF TRUST IN GOD

STARTING FROM THE VERY BEGINNING, GOD DESIGNED THE PINNACLE of his creation, humanity, to rely on him for everything we would need. His instructions in the garden were about faithful (trusting) obedience to his Word. The Fall was about an unwillingness to trust God and his Word, and therefore mankind was cast out of his presence. But in his faithfulness, God continued to work and move in and among his people, refusing to abandon us to the consequences of our own unwillingness to trust him. This culminated in the death and resurrection of Jesus Christ, which offers new life, a fresh start, and a clean relationship with the Spirit's indwelling power to trust God. The residue of the Fall still remains, however, and so in this life we struggle to consistently trust God and his Word. But the constant call of the Word, the Image of God stamped onto the fabric of our souls, and the Spirit's prompting all resound with one chorus: "Trust God! Believe in him. Have faith that he is faithful."

Whenever we fail to heed this call and choose to rebel against its simple yet pervasive message, we cease in that moment and for that time to trust God. We sin. Sin is, essentially, our decision not to trust God and his Word.

Think about a sin that nips at your heels, and consider where it comes from. When's the last time you were really mad at your son and you allowed your anger to cause you to blow it? Maybe he was disrespectful, lied to you, or simply ignored your fatherly mandates. What happened inside you? What caused you to "fall over the edge" and lose out to the power of the anger you felt inside? When my anger wins out and I lash out at my son, I cause pain to him and hurt him in a way that affects my relationship to him. When I calm down, I recognize that even though I may have had a valid reason for experiencing the *emotion* of anger, the way I handled that anger was a failure to trust God with both the circumstance and the powerful emotion.

This is just one area where I turn my back on trusting God and try to take back control of my life. Whenever I do it, I cause pain and broken relationships. Yes, many factors and forces make trust a seemingly impossible response to some circumstances, but it's *still* our responsibility to make the decision to trust God and respond out of what we know to be true. This is what it means to "watch your life and doctrine closely" (1 Timothy 4:16). Over time, as we respond to God working in us as we trust him, the Spirit provides the power to overcome our natural propensity to go our own way. This issue *always* comes down to the object of trust—either myself, which is the essence of sin, or God, which is the goal of discipleship.

I realize I'm in danger of oversimplifying the complex and difficult power that our sinful nature has over us. Our unique histories and personal pathologies do play a part in our personal journeys with Christ. But the power and beauty of the gospel offers three consistent biblical facts:

- I'm a sinner who is personally incapable of healing myself (see Romans 3:23).
- God promises his Spirit to those who are *willing* to trust him (see Romans 8).
- The Spirit provides the means to trust God in a way that produces the quality and character of life that only the Spirit can create (see John 15; Galatians 5).

These three facts summarize the core of the gospel message. They all come down to where I place my trust—or rather, *in whom* I place my trust. But how do we proactively live as truster-disciples?

THE KEYS TO BEING A TRUSTER-DISCIPLE

FOR A FATHER TO NURTURE A SON WHO IS A TRUSTER-DISCIPLE, THREE practical keys must become part of not only his faith, but also who he is.

#1—Filtering Life's Questions Through the Lens of Trust

A truster-disciple knows that nothing occurs in life outside the realm of faith. Every situation, relationship, or decision ultimately comes down to a very straightforward question: What does it mean for me to trust Jesus here and now?

In working with young disciples for nearly three decades, I see that the seeming simplicity of this key has been hard for many to comprehend. A few years ago I was working with Shawn, a sixteen-year-old who confessed to an inability to control his sexual urges. I immediately steered the conversation to his relationship with God in Christ.

"What does Jesus have to do with me and sex, other than telling me it is wrong and he's mad at me? This isn't Jesus' problem, it's *my* problem."

"Sure, it's Jesus' problem, because he loves you. He knows you can't change on your own, and he also knows that a whole lot of issues come together inside you to influence your decisions and life, even when it comes to sex. That's what it means to be a Christian—to trust that he understands what you are going through, that he knows and loves you, and that he's given you his Spirit, who is committed to helping you make progress in your faith. All he asks you to do is to look him in the eye and trust him at his word."

"But," Shawn shot back, "that sounds like a cop-out. It seems like you're telling me God is the one who makes the changes inside me. . . . That doesn't make sense."

"Sure it does, because he's God and you are goofed up, just like me. That's the *point* of why he died and rose again—to live his life through you as you trust him to lead, teach, and guide you."

"But what does *that* mean? Trust him with my sex life? With my girlfriend and *her* sex life?"

"Now you're beginning to get it, Shawn! Yep, take it all to him—your frustrations, your guilt, and your fear of hurting your relationship with him—honestly, with nothing held back. Like almost anything else in life, sex is neither good nor bad; it's neutral. What matters is how we *view* and what we *do* with the issues related to our sexuality. It's how we talk and think and act about sex that shows who we're trusting. When we treat sex like an amusement park ride or something to try to 'get,' we're showing no concern for that person. We abuse ourselves and them for our own

selfish whims and desires. Even if we don't know them—
in a magazine, on a video screen, or someone who sits
across from us in class—when we allow ourselves to go
to sexual thoughts with them, we show our true colors.
We're not trusting that God will meet our needs for meaningful relationships. We're trusting our own selfish hearts,
at a great cost to us and to the other person.

"This is true with your girlfriend too. You might both
believe it's okay or even good to play around with sexual
experiences—even when intercourse isn't involved—but
the choices you are making, as good and right as they *feel,*
are actually destructive to both the relationship and to each
other. This is the biggest reason God has called us to live
"pure" lives—our own desires can so easily destroy others.
God is calling you to choose whom you trust. Do you
believe in God enough to trust him, the one who has
designed the incredible gift of sexual relationship to be
experienced within a lifelong, committed relationship; or
yourself, who enjoys living for now? God knows you, and
he knows your desires and passions. He also knows how
easy it is to break a heart, and a broken heart leads to even
worse consequences down the road."

#2—Evaluating Decisions in Light of Trusting God

This means that the *moral* thing to do must always be dis-
sected according to the question of trust. Every situation
and decision forces us to take one of at least two possible
roads. Which will lead us closer to trusting God and which
will lead us more to trusting ourselves—which is moving
in the opposite direction from God? This fork in the road
will also force the question of love, because that's the core
of the gospel. Discerning the most loving response is never
enough, because we're limited in our ability to see life
from God's perspective. We must align a commitment to
love with a willingness to trust God. This provides the filter the truster-disciple uses to make decisions leading to
growth as a person and as a man of God.

For example, if your son is tempted to drink alcohol

with his friends, his motives are almost always more linked to his longing for community and acceptance than to getting drunk. We fathers often make the mistake of looking at the observable sinful behaviors instead of looking at what's truly happening in the hearts and minds of our sons. Of course, you don't want your son to drink. But the way to help him to make that decision (which is going to be his to make, whether you like it or not) is to talk about what drives him to that behavior. You want to encourage him to be motivated to change his behaviors *not* because he's afraid of you or because he thinks he should rely solely on the notion of "objective morality." Rather, you want to stress that deciding to drink with his buddies demonstrates that he doesn't think God is able to or wants to provide the kind of community and acceptance your son is looking for.

This is true for any moral or ethical question. The choice we make rests on what we believe fulfills the rule of love as well as what causes us to trust God.

#3—Viewing Life in Relational Rather than Performance Terms

My friend Brennan is a speaker and writer who facilitates retreats to help groups experience what it means to live out of an encouraging and intimate faith in God. In one such gathering, he wrapped up a weekend by asking the twelve participants, all lay Christian leaders who had spent a weekend contemplating the passionate love God has for each of them, to close their eyes. Then he asked them to focus on Jesus' expression as they locked eyes with him. After a time of silence, Brennan asked each to describe in one word Christ's expression as he looked at them. Nearly every person, in one way or another, expressed that Jesus seemed disappointed in them. "Yes," one told me later, "God loves me, but he knows me so well and he knows how poorly I'm doing as a Christian. He wants me to do better; that's what I saw in his eyes."

This response represents a heretical disease. God is far more interested in who we *are* and who we are *becoming* than he is in the *doing* of our faith. This can be a tough pill to swallow, because it goes against the grain of what we've heard our whole lives about faith. Most of us do think of God as a lover who is passionately committed to us, but we also think of him standing back watching us live out our commitment, like a coach or a teacher. But he's so much more than a coach or a teacher. He's a friend, a lover, a bridegroom who is constantly on the move to win us into his arms. Yes, God desires our holiness and our behavior to reflect our belief, but he died to reconcile us back into relationship with him, so that he can draw us into a life that *reflects* our faith.

A truster-disciple sees his faith as an ongoing, vibrant, evolving, deepening *relationship* of trusting the God who has first pursued him.

FROM FATHER TO SON

1. Take your son out for a fun time—bowling, movie, tennis— and afterward take time to talk about the latest struggle you had with each other. Talk about how it made each of you feel and why.

2. Take an example from your life and allow your son to hear how difficult it is for you to trust God in this area. (However, avoid any subject that can shake his sense of security in you or your family, such as sexual struggles or intense financial fears.)

3. Ask him to tell you the next time he is tempted not to trust God, and promise him you will not punish him for his honesty. (This may be tough. Never promise this unless you'll follow through.) Talk as a friend about God's view of the issue and how God wants to help him through it. Pray with and for him.

GO FOR IT!

Do a mission trip together without too many people you know—the more impoverished, oppressed, or needy the people you serve are, the better. As you process your experience, discuss how much you possess and how it can be difficult for people who have a lot to trust God. Decide how you'll encourage each other to trust God in new ways.

FROM FATHER TO FATHER

1. After a minute of silent prayer and reflection, have each dad describe in a word how God feels about him. Discuss what's behind these feelings.

2. Take a minute to consider silently your relationships with your sons. Have each father use a word or phrase to describe how each one's son feels about his dad right now. Without violating confidences or making your sons look bad, ask each man to give an example of where his son trusts him and where he doesn't. Talk about why this level of trust exists in each relationship.

CHAPTER 5

THE MARKS OF A DISCIPLE: A FOLLOWER

> Don't become so well-adjusted to your culture that you fit into it without even thinking. Instead, fix your attention on God. You'll be changed from the inside out. Readily recognize what he wants from you, and quickly respond to it. Unlike the culture around you, always dragging you down to its level of immaturity, God brings the best out of you, develops well-formed maturity in you.
>
> —ROMANS 12:2 (MSG)

A FEW YEARS AGO MY WIFE AND I BEGAN THE BOOK *Daughters and Dads* with a story of watching *Father of the Bride* on an airplane. A certain scene had caused me to weep, *in public! On a plane!*

Well, it happened again. And this time it had nothing to do with tapping into the memories of my daughter's childhood. This time I was moved by a different set of emotions. As much as I tried first to avoid it and then to conceal it, I got "weepy" (a rotten but accurate description) watching *Remember the Titans.*

The film is a classic guy's flick, filled with images of strength and conflict as a group of young men band together around a common goal. Due to the merging of two high schools—one primarily African-American and one Caucasian—both football programs are faced with the challenge of forced integration. The film works because the complexity of the racial issues focuses on the players themselves. While there are many scenes that get to me, the one that hits me hardest is when the All-American white player, paralyzed in a car accident, is visited by the star African-American lineman. These guys are the leaders of their respective teams, and their journey of learning to respect one another leads them eventually to express their love for one another. Every time I see this scene I can't help it; the tears start flowing.

In this day of constant motion, perpetual upgrading, and never-ending performance anxiety, what can stir our souls? To ask it another way, What's inside a man's heart that causes him to be touched by compassion, healing, triumph, or the overcoming of evil? I imagine it's different for each of us, but I'm convinced that within each man lies a remnant of passion for what's right, worthy, and honorable. No matter how far we've moved from the beauty of creation, we all still understand the glory of goodness, and we're moved by the power of redemption, honor, and love. This is the thumbprint of God stamped on our souls, indelibly engraved on our hearts.

THE REALITY OF FALLEN HUMANITY

WHAT WE EXPERIENCE IN THE MIDST OF THE DAILY GRIND SEEMS FAR removed from the gallant and selfless acts in the stories we love. In great movies and epic novels, the heroes are heroic and the good is consistently good. But in real life, people are complex, conflicted, and hypocritical. Life often jolts us out of our Hollywood reverie. Everyday life is filled with pain, brokenness, and deep disappointment. People often aren't what they seem to be; the poor and weak get trampled while the cunning and savvy receive rewards. And the older we get, the more we get stuck in the rut of selfish stubbornness and contentious power plays. Life is *anything* but a story celebrating the wonderful, the safe, or the good.

But God set apart the church to be different. Or at least

we're *called* to work hard at being different. The call of God to live as a follower of Jesus Christ is to rise above the slime of an imperfect and fallen world and to "put on the new self, which is being renewed in knowledge in the image of its Creator" (Colossians 3:10). As those who have been redeemed, we have before us a fairly clear-cut choice: to take the low road and live in partnership with the dictates of a broken, sinful culture, or to seek the best of every person we encounter, according to the design of the Great Lover in creation and redemption.

A FOLLOWER-DISCIPLE – A GENTLE WARRIOR FOR CHRIST

MY WIFE'S FAMILY HAS A LONG TRADITION OF GIVING EACH CHILD A special name, apart from the name given at birth, representing who that child is as uniquely created by God. We've carried on this tradition with our children. Our oldest is a fun, passionate, and (appropriately) strong-willed leader on whom we bestowed "Lion Cub." Our daughter, the beautiful dancer who is as graceful with people as she is on stage, has a way of seeing life through the lens of one who knows God, so she is our "Angel Eyes." Our middle son, Rob, combines two very different and unique characteristics, and his name reflects this.

As Rob was growing up, it became evident that he had an exceptionally rare combination of personal strength and deep tenderness, so the name we chose for him was "Gentle Warrior." Our desire has been for the Lord to protect this incredible boy by preserving the best of both sides of his character. He has an intense love for God, a desire to be God's man, and a passion to make a mark in the world. Coupled with this is a rare ability to dance to his own tune in his own way. This combination has made him a powerful person in a world that tries to cram everyone into a specified cultural image. Rob is a gentle warrior, out to battle forces that seek to destroy those whom God loves. Even as he is trying to figure out life as a middle adolescent in the midst of the pressures of school and sports and friends, we see glimpses of who he's becoming. At various times he is a champion of the underdog, a model for the unique, and a leader for those who long for freedom from the chains of conformity.

These characteristics are those of Jesus' disciples. As the apostle Paul reminds us, "Our struggle is not against flesh and blood, but against the rulers, against the authorities, against the powers of this dark world and against the spiritual forces of evil in the heavenly realms" (Ephesians 6:12). To a gentle warrior committed to following Jesus Christ, the enemy is never another human being. The struggle may be corporate—against institutions and organizations that seek to do harm, that oppress and beat down the brokenhearted. Or the struggle may be personal—against behaviors that would do the same. Or the struggle may be spiritual— against powers beyond our comprehension. But a gentle warrior follows Christ into the fray, confounding and confronting any and all powers and influences that seek to cause "one of these little ones . . . to sin." (Matthew 18:6). With single-minded focus, the gentle warrior who follows Christ strives to be as consistent as possible in how he models grace, is an ambassador for peace, and is focused on being a leader who is compelled to offer mercy and justice to others. He's a follower of Christ.

The Holy Spirit plants four kingdom values within your son as he turns his life over to God's reign. For your son to see himself as a gentle warrior—an authentic, passionate, and committed follower-disciple—the following four words provide a picture of his marching orders and life convictions.

Reconciliation

The way most people understand "reconciliation" is as the process that seeks the restoration of a relationship that has been fractured. When the New Testament uses this word, it focuses specifically on the relationship between God and those he has created (see, for example, 2 Corinthians 5:18-20). But this does not let those who are follower-disciples off the hook in terms of relationships with other people.

The life of Jesus and the Bible itself are both consistently clear on this point: to follow Jesus means to be a diligent and dedicated reconciler in a world of broken relationships. God not only wants to reconcile your son to himself; he also calls the follower-disciple to partner with him in bringing his kingdom into every aspect of human existence.

Examples of this abound, especially in the New Testament:

> Therefore each of you must put off falsehood and speak truthfully to his neighbor, for we are all members of one body. (Ephesians 4:25)

> If you have any encouragement from being united with Christ, if any comfort from his love, if any fellowship with the Spirit, if any tenderness and compassion, then make my joy complete by being like-minded, having the same love, being one in spirit and purpose. Do nothing out of selfish ambition or vain conceit, but in humility consider others better than yourselves. Each of you should look not only to your own interests, but also to the interests of others. (Philippians 2:1-4)

A thirty-five-year-old youth pastor named Glen wanted his son to recognize the importance of being a reconciling force. During one particularly painful time in their church, Glen decided to bring his son, Frankie, and two other youth group students to a meeting between some angry elders and his staff. The elders were fed up with the "wild skateboarders who terrorized the adults" going into the midweek Bible study, and they had ordered Glen to ban them from the church property on Wednesday nights. Glen and his team were there to discuss how the entire church could care for these tough neighborhood kids. Sure, Glen agreed, their behavior and language was a problem, but he and his staff were convinced they were making progress. Frankie and his two friends sat on the fringes through most of the meeting and were clearly upset that the elders didn't seem able to listen to the concerns of the youth staff. Glen took a risk: In the middle of an especially heated exchange between an elder and a volunteer leader, he asked his son to pray for peace and understanding. He didn't ask permission to change the course of the meeting; he just did it. Frankie, shy and a bit taken aback, said a simple prayer: "God, you love us, and you love those kids. Teach us how to love as you love. Amen."

Silence.

Finally, an elder spoke. "What should we do, Frankie?"

"Well," Frankie said, "talk to them yourself. Pray for them, then sit down and get to know them. Come to the youth group and listen to them. I think you'll know what to do then."

A gentle warrior was born, and Frankie hasn't been the same since.

As a gentle warrior, your son is called to follow Jesus into the muck of ordinary, messy relationships. As a follower-disciple he is commissioned with the responsibility to be God's hands, feet, and mouthpiece. He is the "aroma of Christ" (2 Corinthians 2:15), and as Philip Yancey put it, "a dispenser of grace" to the world. The gentle warrior is one who seeks to bring together those who have been separated.

Inclusion
God has no room in his economy for someone who abuses power and privilege, who sees himself as distinct or separate from others, or who creates a we/they world. Yet across denominational and theological lines, far too many people, in their own desire for power, recognition, or quest, exclude others. As fathers, we know this is as natural as breathing. The stronger our convictions, the easier it is to slip into an "I'm right; they're idiots" mode. As hard as it is to admit, I know I'm responsible for planting at least a little of this spirit in my boys. Yet the Bible gives me no wiggle room here. "God is love" and the fruit of the Spirit is "kindness, goodness, gentleness . . ." Ouch! We must

help our sons to see that the true follower-disciple is called to go against the flow and love everyone.

One biblical example of this is how we treat those who are different from us socially. James argues this point in terms of economic exclusionism:

> My brothers, as believers in our glorious Lord
> Jesus Christ, don't show favoritism. Suppose a
> man comes into your meeting wearing a gold ring
> and fine clothes, and a poor man in shabby
> clothes also comes in. If you show special atten-
> tion to the man wearing fine clothes and say,
> "Here's a good seat for you," but say to the poor
> man, "You stand there" or "Sit on the floor by my
> feet," have you not discriminated among your-
> selves and become judges with evil thoughts?
>
> Listen, my dear brothers: Has not God chosen
> those who are poor in the eyes of the world to
> be rich in faith and to inherit the kingdom he
> promised those who love him? But you have
> insulted the poor. Is it not the rich who are
> exploiting you? Are they not the ones who are
> dragging you into court? Are they not the ones
> who are slandering the noble name of him to
> whom you belong?
>
> If you really keep the royal law found in
> Scripture, "Love your neighbor as yourself," you
> are doing right. But if you show favoritism, you
> sin and are convicted by the law as lawbreakers.
> (James 2:1-9)

Exclusion takes many forms. We may exclude others because of their social status. But we also may exclude oth-ers because they don't worship like we do, think exactly like we do, or believe the exact same things we do. We're all prone to want to separate from the pack; that's a part of our base nature: We want to connect in community but our fallenness also wants to set up the Great Us as being better than, smarter than, or more holy than everyone else.

Stan and Debbie have committed their lives to sharing Christ with international leaders in business and government. They've raised their three children to respect different worldviews and perspectives, trying to teach them to follow the example of Paul:

> Do not cause anyone to stumble, whether Jews, Greeks or the church of God—even as I try to please everybody in every way. For I am not seeking my own good but the good of many, so that they may be saved. Follow my example, as I follow the example of Christ. (1 Corinthians 10:32–11:1)

As his son was growing up, Stan looked for any opportunity he could find to expose Jerry to different people and perspectives. After these encounters, Stan took Jerry out to talk with him about the person they'd just met. Even when Jerry was in his early teen years, they'd discuss how to be a follower of Christ, even in the presence of someone who disagreed on tightly held convictions, whether doctrinal, political, or social. As his son grew, Jerry planted in him the importance of love and inclusion, and helped him to navigate the difficult and complicated struggles that commitment brings. Today in his mid-twenties, Jerry is a passionate gentle warrior who is actively committed to spreading the gospel to those who haven't yet heard about the love of Christ.

A follower-disciple is a warrior out to change anything that divides the body of Christ. A father who teaches his son to be a gentle warrior addresses division by being a man who's inclusive of all who walk with God and a man who compassionately engages all who don't. This doesn't mean he compromises the essence of the gospel for the sake of warm feelings and safe relationships. It does mean, however, that he seeks to include into his circle of love those God includes. According to the gospel, that includes everyone: "God our Savior . . . wants all men to be saved and to come to a knowledge of the truth" (1 Timothy 2:3-4). After all, Jesus modeled compassionate honesty; he always spoke truth yet never ceased to love with great passion and focus. The follower-disciple is committed to making room for authentic differences but maintains an authentic commitment to drawing people together in the name of Jesus Christ.

Trustworthiness

Earlier we talked about trusting God as an important mark of a disciple. But what about trust between people? What does it mean for your son to be a follower-disciple who is trustworthy?

Trust seems to be a rare commodity these days. Someone who is *worthy* of trust is even more rare. Proverbs tells us, "A wicked messenger falls into trouble, but a trustworthy envoy brings healing" (13:17). One dictionary defines a trustworthy person as being "worthy of the total confidence in the integrity, ability, and good character of another."[1] Trust becomes one of the most important discipleship issues in both the spiritual development and the personal development of your son. In most of our relationships, once we break a confidence it takes a great deal to rebuild trust. A broken trust has a long memory, and sometimes we even do irreparable damage when we break a trust. Whether in a friendship, the workplace, or the church, the ability to trust another is something to be held sacred.

As a follower-disciple, the gentle warrior must be committed to the kind of integrity that engenders trust. For most people the breech of trust itself isn't the primary source of broken confidence. When all is said and done, the spirit and attitude of the person is the most significant factor in healing broken trust and confidence. We all fail—our friends, our coworkers, even our spouses. We've all let others down, and we've all violated another's trust in us. But a trustworthy man who follows Christ is the first to confess, to run and ask forgiveness, and to seek help in learning how to grow through failure when he falls short of being trustworthy.

Cliff is one of my heroes. He's one of those rare guys

who are brutally honest but incredibly gentle. Cliff caught his son in a lie when he was thirteen. Cliff did what great fathers do; he discussed the pain he felt when lied to and shared how slippery and dangerous a journey of deceit can be. He also let his son know that the consequences for breaking trust and lying would be less severe if he came clean and told the truth before Cliff and his wife found out about it.

The next week, when Cliff was driving his son to a practice, he was pulled over for speeding. Without thinking, he told the officer that he had no idea he was speeding and that—although he was clocked at twelve miles over the speed limit—he was *sure* his speedometer read only three or four over. The officer gave him just a warning. Driving away, Cliff breathed a sigh of relief. His son, however, sat fuming, because he knew that his dad was a habitual speeder. Cliff, feeling guilty but stubborn, tried to ignore his son as he dropped him off.

That night, after some time to realize what he'd done, Cliff went into his son's room and asked his forgiveness for lying. But he went on. He asked his son what he thought he should do about it. His son repeated back to him the speech his father had given him, about the "slippery slope of lying" and how eventually that kind of life can hurt a lot of people. He told Cliff that he thought he should make it right. Then he added, "Good night, Dad. I love you."

The next day Cliff went to the police station and tried to get a ticket. They refused. Still, Cliff knew that his son had just taken a giant leap in understanding what it means to be a trustworthy man of God.

Trustworthiness is where your son may need the most training and probably the clearest modeling. He has to know that becoming a man of integrity who can be trusted means accepting his weaknesses, confessing his shortcomings and failures, and being willing to learn from his mistakes.

Honesty

Studies show that 80 percent of adolescents lie, and the other 20 percent don't tell researchers the truth.

In general, two primary factors cause a lack of integrity at this stage of life. First, from about thirteen or fourteen years old to the late teens, an adolescent is neither child nor adult. For more than a hundred years, we've identified this as a stage of life where neither category adequately describes where an adolescent is. "Not quite child but not yet adult" is the closest we can come to describing the person we're raising. He's only *developing* his sense of self, his *identity*. He hasn't yet landed on who he perceives himself to be. During these years (mid-adolescence), most kids are several years away from recognizing and accepting who they are. Their focus is solely on protecting themselves and meeting their own needs, dreams, and desires. Because of this, to the child, lying is often not seen as *lying,* because objective truth is still abstract.

This may sound like a weak justification for immoral and irresponsible behavior. In part, it is! But recognizing that lying is a developmentally driven behavior will help you at least to be able to understand that for your son to be honest, he must swim hard upstream against the tide of other adolescents. Yes, it's appropriate and necessary to expect and demand honesty. But when you overreact to violations of this expectation, you drive your son into feeling like he's being forced to live two lives—one with his friends and the other at home. Honest communication and clear consequences couched in a willingness to understand will help your son grow through the pressures to deceive.

Second, we live with a culture that treats truth and integrity as relative and subjective, convincing our kids (and even us) that the concept of "my truth" rather than a commitment to "the truth" is adequate. Your son may want to tell the truth and commit to a consistency of integrity, but it's essentially impossible. Does this mean we give into this developmental and cultural tidal wave? Of course not! We simply try to understand what we're up against. But for the follower of Jesus Christ, a commitment to try to live the truth and a lifestyle of integrity is central to the journey.

LIFE AS A FOLLOWER-DISCIPLE

NO MATTER HOW MANY TIMES I'VE WATCHED *REMEMBER THE Titans,* I continue to be deeply moved by the goodness and triumph in the story. I believe such emotional responses come from God's image stamped on our souls. God has created us to walk together with him to bring healing and wholeness to creation. The Fall convinced us we were better off alone, fighting and biting and devouring one another. But the Cross and Resurrection restored the original intent of our Redeemer in the hearts of those who love him. We're created to follow Jesus Christ and to love others as he first loved us—with integrity and truth. We *know* this in our hearts, and it's why we're emotionally stirred when people stand up and choose love.

Your son knows this as well. God stamped it on his heart too. And he's waiting for you to teach him how to live this out as the foundational principle of his faith in God. You play a crucial role in helping him to grow into a follower-disciple of Jesus Christ. You are (and always will be) a vital teacher, leader, guide, and friend in his pursuit of faith. God has set before you a dynamic opportunity and a frightening challenge: to help your son to recognize that he was created for a single purpose—to follow Jesus Christ with single-minded commitment and devotion. In the final analysis, he *isn't* called to follow his hopes, dreams, and ambitions. Rather, he is called to follow Jesus and to filter all of life through that central relationship.

This core principle needs to be your focus as you share your life in Christ with your son. During his adolescent journey, his behaviors will probably be irregular at best and destructive at worst. But that does not mean he's rejected you or Christ. Even for the healthiest and most committed young man, becoming a mature follower-disciple is a lifelong journey. We're all on this journey. Your modeling and progress is what matters in the long run.

FROM FATHER TO SON

1. Include your son in discussions with other adults about how people think, act, or believe differently. Discuss with him what it means to love others and still remain true to the integrity of the gospel.

2. Find at least one passage of Scripture that encourages each of the four areas discussed in this chapter—reconciliation, inclusion, trustworthiness, and integrity—and memorize them together.

3. Give your son a new responsibility to develop his trustworthiness. (Some ideas: a checking account, planning a family outing, doing family chores.)

GO FOR IT!

The next time a significant issue involves your church, find a way to get your son involved in it. You may encounter resistance from other adults who don't think a young man has much to offer, especially with tough or complex issues. But as you lead your son to follow Christ, he needs to know that part of his calling is to wade into difficult waters. Of course, don't toss him into the fray alone, but enter with him and maintain his involvement in the issue as a poignant, teachable moment in his young life.

FROM FATHER TO FATHER

1. What films emotionally move you? Analyze what causes you to be touched? If you're not emotionally affected by movies, what gets to you emotionally? If you can't think of a specific setting where your emotions are tapped, can you discuss or identify why?

2. Which of the four areas mentioned in this chapter (reconciliation, inclusion, trustworthiness, or integrity) is the easiest to pass on to your son in his faith journey? Which is the hardest? Why?

3. Where did your father or an important father figure most clearly model God's plan for you in these areas? Where did his relationship with you negatively impact your ability to follow Jesus in these areas?

PART II

FROM FATHER TO SON:
MAINTAINING FOCUS

How We Go After It:
The Goals of Discipleship

My will is my glory; it is also what gives me the most trouble. . . . The question at the heart of the intersection of God's will and human wills is apparently at the heart of everything. The relation of God's will and my will is not a specialized religious question; it is *the* question. The way we answer it shapes our humanity in every dimension.

—EUGENE PETERSON

MOST MEN ARE FAIRLY ADEPT AT SETTING GOALS IN A WORK SETting. The average guy recognizes that it's vital to have a driving purpose and clear objective in the dog-eat-dog world of commerce. Few of us have the luxury of showing up for work and simply punching a timecard, having someone else think for us, plan for us, and make necessary adjustments as we go about our work. In most environments, goal setting and being driven by a larger purpose dictate our decisions and actions.

But we tend to leave that requirement at the office. We come home to rest, to relax, and to enjoy life. We want our family members to love us as we love them and to recognize the home as a place of safety and sanctuary. Our homes and our families are often the only environment where we feel safe and free to be ourselves, to let down, and to avoid the pressures of strategy and visionary reflection.

Once a child enters your life, home is much more than that. Becoming a parent means *you're* the one who must ensure your home is a place of safety, refuge, and nurture for your children. Your home becomes the place where you must do your best strategic and decisive work. The office and boss may *expect* you to give a hundred percent for the good of the company. But in the grand scheme of life this is play-acting stuff compared to the responsibility of nurturing and shaping life in the context of family. Other influences matter in your child's development, but no other person has anywhere near your influence as a parent.

The older your kids get, the harder (and less effective in the long run) parental goal-setting becomes. When your children are little, you can come home from work, kiss them, play for a few minutes, and then sit down to read the mail or watch the news. But when your oldest hits about twelve, the game begins to change.

During childhood, "the family" is what defines our sons. If there's a nurturing and safe environment, relative relational stability in the home, and time and opportunity to explore life, a son can receive all he needs. But as soon as he hits that stage of life known as adolescence, he leaves behind the role of child and sets out on a quest for independence. A parent, and especially a father, needs to know what his role is during this time. We've already looked at the "marks of a disciple." Now we'll turn to the goals of discipleship when it comes to leading, nurturing, and caring for an adolescent. These goals must remain in the forefront of every decision, rule, boundary, discussion, and conflict.

How do we help our sons bring together their wills with God's? Do we "break the will" of our sons to fill them with God's will? As tempting at times as this approach may be, a son who has come to faith by having his will broken doesn't have the inner staying power to achieve the desired goal of discipleship: a lifelong journey of committed love and obedience to Christ. It may even be possible that breaking someone's will could cause him to lack the internal strength to make decisions on his own. This approach could also produce a young man who sees faith as a process of sitting back as an observer, waiting for God to will and to rule, without that grand scheme having any connection to his dreams, passions, or desires.

This isn't faith. It's sanctified resignation.

One alternative—training a son to consider life and faith as if the entire enterprise rests on *him* and his ability to please a distant God—is just as bad. This not-so-subtle discipleship tack is akin to communicating that God has done his work, so now it's your turn. But even a whisper of this perspective in raising a son to love God produces the kind of external faith that leaves the inner soul lonely and cold.

Neither of these extremes even begins to capture the partnership God invites us into in the great dance of life. The God of creation is anything but passionless and uninvolved. He's the Great Dancer who has invaded human history with little fanfare but great ambition—to woo the affection of those he loves. The Lord of the Scriptures is on a quest to take your son on a journey that results in the melding of his will with the kingdom. A dad's role is to help his child live as an active participant in God's design for him and to acknowledge Christ's activity in both his life and the world. This response to the God who wills the best for your son is the central objective of the discipleship task and process.

The four goals listed in this section, then, represent what a response to God's in-breaking love and kingdom work can look like. They may not be the final list, but they do summarize what it means to dance through life as a lover, relater, truster, and follower of Jesus Christ.

Finally, the most significant idea to keep in mind as you continue reading is this: *Parenthood is not a sprint, it is a marathon . . . and the small, insignificant wins and even the temporary losses are not nearly as important as a strong finish.*

CHAPTER 6

GOAL #1:
TO LIVE FROM THE INSIDE OUT

As we learn to live in confidence that the deepest
concerns of our soul are in good hands, both the
shame we feel because of our unworthiness and the
terror we have of one day facing exposure and rejection will lose their power to control us. Change from
the inside out involves a gradual shift away from self-
protective relating to strongly loving involvement.

—LARRY CRABB

THIS MORNING I WAS ON A CROWDED SHUTTLE ON MY WAY TO THE
airport when a man came running out of the hotel trying to get his family on the shuttle. He hustled his wife and
two sons—probably eight to ten years old—onto the bus
while he retrieved the luggage. Although I was sitting next
to these kids, I didn't think twice about them. They were
just two boys waiting for their dad. Then I noticed their
frayed baseball hats, mismatched clothes, rumpled hair,
and dirty socks. I smiled, reflecting on the fact that they
were just being what they looked like—normal boys.

I thought about my boys at that age. I pictured my own
sons on a hotel shuttle, and I remembered some of my
own feelings whenever I was with them in public. As I sat
on that shuttle a horrible thought hit me like a hammer. In
situations like this, I was often a controlling and sometimes
even harsh father concerned about the state of their hair,

the curve of their hat bills, or the general state of their appearance. I rarely enjoyed the fact that they were my unique and precious boys, appropriately playing their socially adorned role (just like almost every other boy). I recalled being in similar situations with my oldest son when I would "get into it" with him about how he looked. Looking at these two boys, I was struck with the simple but undeniable reality that most of the time I was hard on my sons because of what they wore or how they looked; no one else saw them with as critical an eye as I did. In retrospect, I'm now certain that other adults saw my boys as normal, fairly well-behaved, attractive kids. For some reason, I couldn't see that. Instead, I was generally worried that they didn't look the way I wanted them to look.

Unfortunately, my attitude wasn't limited to the state of their clothing or their general appearance. It spilled over into their behavior and performance. Part of the reason I'm writing this is confessional, as I've only recently recognized these attitudes and behaviors within myself. More important, what I offer here is a mirror for other dads. The careful eye we use to evaluate and lead our boys needs to be tempered by a healthy dose of reality and grace when it comes to day-to-day living. A ripped hat or dirty socks might upset us. But in the grand scheme of things, almost no one else is thinking anything other than "that's how boys are."

Is it possible you're a bit like me—overly concerned by what's happening on the outside? As fathers, we face the danger of creating an environment where our sons are more concerned with how they look or how they please us than with nurturing and developing what's going on inside. I think most of us know in our heads that behavior and choices are ultimately a reflection of what's going on somewhere deep in the soul. But we easily forget that when we feel compelled to correct or criticize our sons, especially when we're embarrassed or angry. While necessary correction is a loving response to inappropriate behavior, our correction or criticism about external behaviors can also contribute to our sons' belief that the only way for them to survive life is to live it on the outside. This is precisely what we need to avoid. If we don't, they'll develop walls of emotional callus that will become hard to penetrate as they get older.

During his childhood and adolescence is when you have the greatest chance to shape your son one way or another. Either he'll have the confidence to go after life—especially his life in Christ—with the freedom and passion to live out of conviction and truth (from the inside out). Or he'll become a calculated and safe but spiritually stifled, immature believer.

WHAT'S THE BIG DEAL WITH THE "INSIDE"?

THE SINGLE MOST IMPORTANT QUESTION YOUR SON WILL ASK HIMself throughout his teen years is, "Who am I?" Inside he'll intuitively become more aware that he's going through a time in his life when he's no longer a child, that he must make crucial decisions about his life, and that he's ultimately on his own. As he traverses this tightrope between childhood and adulthood, he's constantly on the lookout for anyone or anything that will bring him a sense of safety and comfort. Nearly every issue he faces will come down to a few simple questions inside of him:

- Where do I fit?
- Does anyone really *care* about who I am and that I am here?
- Is this place safe enough for me to spread my wings, for me to really be me?

Whenever your son dreams, plays, talks, laughs, pouts, argues, or fights, he's trying to work out where he fits on the grand stage of life. During his adolescence, this question will be a constant source of fear, loneliness, and frustration. This struggle for his identity is a process he must go through in order to become a healthy, whole adult.

What makes this tough in today's culture is that, as a society, we've allowed ourselves to be fooled into thinking that discovering our identity means trying on various layers of selves, hoping to land on someone we can become. Your son will probably translate that into a need to create a layer of protection between his authentic and true self and the various roles, behaviors, and activities he learns to hide behind. As a father intent on helping your son to grow into the man God has designed him to be, the challenge before you is as straightforward as it is daunting. You need to lead, equip, and encourage your son to fight against any forces that seek to push him into a self that's not who God intends him to be and to resist the temptation to hide behind a self-protective curtain. Put bluntly, this is tough going for the both of you.

That's why, in addition to what your *son* needs, his journey begins with a question for *you:* "Who are you, Dad?" Are you simply a product of the series of events that have shaped you? Are you a consortium of many roles that you've played over the years? Or is there an authentic "you" deeply buried behind the walls of duty and others' expectations? More pointedly, how accessible is your inner self when outside voices are telling you how to live, what to do, and who you are?

This is so crucial as you raise your son, and he'll need much more than an occasional glimpse at the real you. He needs to be able to connect with you at the deepest levels. How do you help your son to become a unique, godly man convinced of who he is from the inside out without showing that this is also happening in you? This is where the real task of godly fathering begins—with the inner journey of faith and identity of the father himself.

MY STORY

I REMEMBER SITTING THROUGH A BORING LECTURE IN COLLEGE where the professor unenthusiastically declared that people are like onions; when you peel away the layers, what you end up with is only a bunch of onion leaves. "This is what's wrong with people today," he pronounced. "They're trying to 'look for themselves' and what they're looking for doesn't exist. People are just a product of their gene pool influenced by their environment."

A few years later, in graduate school, I heard a psychologist basically agree by describing identity as something we try on through our life until we eventually find ourselves as a mixture of various roles and identities that make up the true us. According to these lofty sages, identity is no more than something we test out and eventually wear like a cloak.

Raised in a fairly typical home environment, I learned how to do this well. I put into practice what I'd seen and heard everywhere around me, often with great success. To get others to affirm and welcome me, I defined myself according to my abilities, talents, and accomplishments. Who I was soon became a conglomeration of various selves and roles that I put on and took off like masks. When I found I could be funny, I was happy about my life. When I was involved in a sport, I played that role. When I was at a Young Life meeting or at church, I switched my persona and became a more focused, more spiritually inclined leader. When I was with my closest friends, I was somewhat able to sync my various roles together. But throughout much of my life, even this was difficult, because I had so little internal understanding of who the real me actually was. I never thought much about it, not consciously anyway. I simply did my best to make my mark and create a self who was relatively safe wherever I went.

But somewhere deep inside me, I knew there was more to life. More specifically, I knew there was more to *me*. As much as I tried to live life on the outside, I was constantly hounded by this small, fragile self who was in constant motion—thinking, reacting, responding, and navigating the labyrinth of life as a young man. I knew a soul was buried deep within me, but I did everything I could to live as if it were weak, powerless, and subject to forces outside of itself. I was driven by the illusion that to discover who I truly was I had to constantly be on the lookout for those performance markers that were continually changing. I was doomed to a never-ending cycle of having to prove myself by what I did, what I controlled or influenced, and what others said about me.

Years later, I discovered the truth about my identity. I believed in God and loved others as best I knew how, but seeing myself as unique and valuable on the inside because God calls me his own was very foreign to me. For the last ten or so years, I've been on a difficult journey to listen to the encouraging voice of God calling me his precious son, and realizing that I will find my true self—my identity—only when I allow myself to trust that voice. My quest to discover my identity is a call to let go of the lies of culture that gauge my worth, value, and sense of self by what I do, what I control, or what others say about me.

My role as a dad, then, has been to do everything in my power to encourage the person God created to burst forth in each of my sons. The voices they constantly hear—be good, be successful, be consistent, be strong, be manly—are the same messages that seek to push my sons down. These may not be bad advice as general expressions of what it means to stand tall as men. But when I sense even a hint of danger that either of my sons may try to find himself by allowing those voices to cause him to live life on the outside, I *must* step in. This is your role too: to create the kind of environment where your son learns how to listen to God's voice, to look within himself in order to discover who he is. The trick is helping your son to set free the person God created, loves, and has already declared free. This is what it means to live life from the inside out.

I'm telling you my story because it deeply affects my role as a father. When I'm honest, I realize I'm a cauldron of contradiction, a split-personality mess who can't seem to get life straight. Sometimes I'm able to bless my sons and set them free to live from the inside as God's chosen men. But at other times I push too hard about their performance, unceasingly grilling them about their grades or challenging their decisions in ways that stifle their growth and unwittingly encourage unhealthy dependence on me. I want to and need to hold their feet to the fire to lead them as God has called me to. But I have to be equally concerned that the way I talk to, listen to, and lead my sons helps them to live life on the inside. I want life for each of my sons to be different than it has been for me. I want him to be successful, and I want others to like him. But most of all, I want him to live out of a sense of freedom and security in the person God has created him to be. I'm sure you want the same for your son.

WHAT ABOUT YOU, DAD?

WHERE ARE YOU WITH THIS? IS THIS A TOPIC THAT MAKES SENSE TO you as a man and as a believer? Do you struggle with trying to live in authentic, abandoned freedom from the inside, or are you just trying to survive the complexities of life day to day? For most guys, this is tough, honest stuff. It's hard. We have jobs, mortgages, and marriages that take our energy. We're expected to live up to a multitude of expectations others have for us. In our frustration, we cry out, "Just tell me what to *do,* and I'll do it!"

But your son needs much, much more than that. He deserves more. He needs you to take the time and effort to do the hard work of self-reflection, so you can teach him how to live from the center of his soul. Paul told Timothy, "Watch your life and doctrine closely. Persevere in them, because if you do, you will save both yourself and your hearers" (1 Timothy 4:16). Your son needs to know that your faith is more about childlike trust than it is about simply surviving the onslaught of life. He needs to know that *you* know what it means to live life from the center.

LIVING FROM THE CENTER

GOD CREATED YOU AND YOUR SON, AND HE CREATED YOU BOTH with a unique stamp of his divine hand. "God spoke" and out of love, new life began. God spoke and your son was born. God spoke and his little frame burst forth, full of life and hope and promise. This same Creator is also the Great Redeemer, an incarnate invader who's not willing to stand by and watch his beloved child fall away from his love. In creation and redemption, the God of all nations and tribes shouts from the heavens that each person is uniquely made and intimately cherished. That's what makes me who I am. It brings a final answer to the question that's held me captive all these years: Am I loved? This is the core truth that will allow your son to experience life from the inside out with his God, in step with the Father's original design for your boy.

To you this may sound strange, even a bit unorthodox. But your task is to live out of that place where you are truly yourself. Your own fallen humanity, the bruises you still feel, the fractures you've suffered, and the disappointments you've encountered, all converge as a voluminous barrage of experiences that seek to rip you from your internal safe haven. Add to this the constant lies that remind you how unworthy you are to be called God's precious son.

It's easy to see why we're so afraid to show any weakness at all. Every time I fail, every time I am criticized, and with each slip on the ladder of power, I can feel myself listening to those voices seeking to make me live on the outside. But the truth is that I am God's precious and loved son. Like the prodigal's father in Luke 15, my King has run into the fields to welcome me home, and when I let myself rest in his embrace, I know I'm free. I can talk and think and pray and lead with a solid sense of purpose and destiny, knowing I'm at my best and have the most to offer as I authentically live from the center of my soul.

HELPING YOUR SON LIVE FROM THE CENTER

What would you say is the primary goal of raising a son? After more than two decades of wrestling with that question, I have come to the place where I honestly believe that the only thing that really matters is to do whatever I can to raise a son who knows and follows God. My goal for each of my sons is for him to honestly trust that he's the beloved of his heavenly Father and that he's cherished for who he is and not for what he accomplishes. Is this your goal as well? It means helping him to view life as an inside-out adventure. Teaching your son to live from the inside out means you need to help him to recognize that real life is experienced from the center and to be convinced that God has called him "out of darkness into his wonderful light" (1 Peter 2:9).

How do you help your son in this process? Or, more accurately, what can you do in partnership with the Spirit to lead your son into a deeper, more effectual relationship with Jesus Christ? Henri Nouwen came to the conclusion that three activities, which he considered "the spiritual disciplines for my life as the chosen one,"[2] helped him to live from that inner place of refuge. These are perhaps the most important spiritual activities for developing a son who knows God and walks intimately with him.

#1—Encourage and Empower Self-Expression

As your son grows, one of the most important things you can do is encourage and empower him to allow what's inside to emerge. As you listen to and observe him, he'll give hints as to who he is on the inside. Whether expressed in a long-term dedicated passion or a flippant one-line desire, your job is to ask questions, to separate childish whims from childlike dreams, and to provide opportunities for your son to explore life. This may not sound very spiritual, but creating this environment will make it safe for him to explore his faith and his gifts when the time comes for them to emerge. Your son must believe that, regardless of how crazy his ideas may sound, he has your blessing to attack life with abandon from the inside out.

Cultivating this inner emotional and spiritual strength can present an interesting dilemma for parents. You may pray for and strategize how to create an environment where your son is able to develop within himself a well of confidence and security, yet it's no fun to parent an adolescent who's stretching his wings. Even if you're tempted to decry the strong-willed child God gave you to raise, or if your formerly gentle and compliant boy is starting to assert himself a little too forcefully in the family, don't let temporary heartaches like these (and a multitude of others you'll surely encounter) discourage you. Developing a strong inner sense of self is a great thing, as long as your son's strength comes from seeing himself as God's beloved son.

Inner strength from the Spirit will eventually create a decisive selflessness; and as he grows, it will rarely be seen as rudeness or arrogance. Your son may at times appear to be both of these things and more, but that's not necessarily bad during his adolescent years. Inner confidence, motivated and driven by your son's part in the kingdom of God, won't look very refined for perhaps decades. But as you help keep your son focused on Jesus and his purposes in the world, his apparent arrogance and selfish strength will become increasingly aligned with God's gentleness, patience, and kindness.

As your son seeks to live from the inside, this kind of living will help him to know who he is and who it is he serves. He'll become less self-focused and more aware that as God leads him, he doesn't need to unjustly project his needs or desires onto others. When he lives out of the center, where he can acknowledge his pain, he can freely love others without self-focused scheming or selfish ambition. Your son can engage in others' sorrows or wanderings because he's already certain that he's been accepted and adored by God himself. This is what it means to live from the center, that place where God the Spirit lives and works to conform us into the image of the Son.

#2—Help to Unmask the World for What It Is and Does

When my boys were growing up, I blew it pretty badly when it came to communicating their worth. I'd begun a practice of rewarding soccer goals with milk shakes on the way home, mostly because my older son was built by God to score, so it seemed like a fun and natural way to celebrate. My younger son, however, has only begun to come into his own as an athlete as a junior in high school. When he was younger, he wasn't very competitive and ended up playing defense in every sport he tried. On the way home from a game one day, my then seven-year-old, four-season soccer veteran son reminded me of my stupidity. As we passed McDonald's, he said, "I guess I'll *never* win a milk shake, huh, Dad?"

Ouch. All the encouragement, pep talks, and fatherly love I poured on my son during those years could not undo one simple fact: he knew he was somehow less than his older brother because he'd never scored a goal and had never "won" a milk shake—and the future looked as dim as the present. Perhaps even worse, my older son had become aware of the direct connection between reward and performance, and realized that to stay top-dog on Dad's list he had to keep forging ahead—even at the expense of other team members.

Don't argue too much here—this is far too important a principle. Sure, life is about performance and reward, and there's no escaping that. But what most fathers fail to recognize is that in order to even begin to live from the center, a son must be firmly convinced that at the end of the day— when the lights are off and the cheering has died down— there's a place where he's safe, loved, and cherished for *who he is*. Of course, celebration, acknowledgment, and reward are appropriate in helping your son learn to appreciate success for what it is. But if he sees his life as mostly an up-and-down cycle of reward and failure, he'll fall into the pressure to live from the outside in.

Instead, your son needs to be reminded regularly that the world is lying when it tells him life is found in success, awards, and accomplishments. He needs to grow up knowing that life is a laboratory for discovering and uncovering who he his, what he loves, and what he's wired to be about. Along the way he'll succeed and receive praise, and he'll fail and be ignored or even scorned. He needs to be convinced that the successes and failures are not about *him* but about the journey of discovery. Your job is to teach him to somehow celebrate life in the midst of the journey—maybe with a milk shake to contemplate both the error and the home run, or just the joy of the game, or the new friends on the team. That's the perspective he needs, especially from you as his father.

You go after this by ensuring an open line of communication so you can discuss both the good and the bad and put them in their proper places of significance. Most of the time, you need to be ready when *your son* is ready to talk. The older he gets, the later at night these discussions seem to occur. But this is a wonderful time when you can remind your son that he is loved and that it makes no difference that he won't start next week, or that he always has to play right field, or that God didn't design him to be a quarterback. "None of this changes anything about who you are," you need to tell him, over and over again. He's designed for and good at many, many things. The joy of life is in the *living*.

#3—Surround Him with People Who Will Bless Him

A whole new body of developmental psychology is looking at the development of what is called adolescent "moral identity." These researchers are trying to find out why certain kids are highly moral in their behavior and why the vast majority are not. What they've discovered is that young people who have received the same positive messages from a wide variety of sources—parents, neighbors, school, sports, church—tend to respond to this barrage of encouragement by taking a higher moral road than the majority of their peers. The others, in contrast, who don't receive the same message but experience conflicting values and moral messages, tend to be more selfish, less involved with others, and less willing to sacrifice anything for anyone. The concept of consistent positive messages from a number of different sources is referred to as "congruence."

The more you think about the impact of congruence on an adolescent, the more obvious it seems. Yet we've never really labeled it before. Throughout history, kids have *not* been raised just by a mother and a father, but rather in the context of an entire community, which often included extended family. There was never any real distance between the values and behaviors of parents and that of school officials or coaches, for they were simply all members of a community that held itself together with a common set of rules and norms.

Today kids desperately need adult influences and relationships that provide congruence. Not all the messages kids hear need to line up *exactly,* but a few of the more significant ones must. For example, for your son to experience congruence, he'll need not only parents, but also a neighbor or two, perhaps a coach or a teacher, a youth ministry program, and other families (or extended family) to all come together in one message of support. This choir has just one refrain: "You are the beloved, not for what you do or how you look, but because God calls you blessed." To convince him of this truth, your son needs to hear and feel and experience the warm chords of this tune throughout his life. Make it your mission to be sure that he has several people in his life who reinforce this basic truth as often as possible.

Partly by accident and partly by design, our kids have several adults that see them as almost their own. Joe, a twenty-one-year-old junior high volunteer still calls Rob (a high school junior) to play golf and to talk; Chuck, a twenty-nine-year-old seminary student, drops by late at night when he knows Chap is back in town from school; and Jeff, a two-decade-plus friend, seeks out our boys simply to encourage them about their lives. These and several other men and women are committed to being a tangible blessing in the lives of our boys. Our sons have yet to fully recognize what a gift these people are to them, but the relational commitment of these adults has dramatically shaped Rob and Chap's faith and life, providing additional models of what it means to live life from the inside out.

#4—Help Him Celebrate His Chosenness Through Gratitude

You probably know this already, but I'll say it anyway: It's very tough in this day of adolescent entitlement to teach our kids to be grateful for everything they have. The entire advertising industry is designed to create a craving for more and better. This means we must work hard as parents to maintain the delicate dance between want and need as well as between careful planning and impulsive consuming.

This said, there are simple ways to take this beyond the obvious issue of spending and "stuff." Here are a few ideas for modeling and instilling in your son a deeply rooted sense of gratitude:

- Pray together at least once a day, probably before a meal. While some argue that a rigid practice can evolve into a meaningless ritual, authentic family prayer is a powerful reminder of our dependence on God. The content, form, and style of prayer should change to keep it fresh, but turning to God is foundational for reminding your family that you all belong to God. This will plant in your son the reminder that God is the source of all good things.

- Before you make any major decision—whether financial, physical, or logistical—talk together as a family about God's intent for your family. Discuss God's desire to take care of you and guide you. When we moved from Colorado to Los Angeles several years ago, we allowed each family member to have a vote. In fact, each person almost had veto power. That was a bit risky with kids who were fifteen, twelve, and nine at the time. But we wanted them to know they each mattered to us and to God. We decided that if God were going to convince one of us to move, he was certainly capable of touching all of us. As it turned out, even though the move was fairly rough, all three kids knew that they had voted to come and that God was in it.

- When you receive a reward or other good thing, talk about God's blessing and how he loves to tangibly remind us that he's involved in our lives and that he looks for ways to encourage us. Dee is in a class by herself when it comes to celebration, and she's constantly on the lookout for reasons to celebrate God's blessings. Our kids have grown up knowing that there's never anything too small or insignificant that it doesn't deserve balloons, streamers, and a special meal. Whether it's the day Rob had his first start in high school football or when Chap bought his truck, we had a wild family time. When we celebrate, we celebrate in Jesus' name, and our kids know it.

- Make it a morning ritual to remind each person in your household to look for God's good work today and then talk about it that night. I have a friend who e-mails his children whenever he's traveling. When he's gone, his son even wakes up early to print out the e-mail before he goes to school.

Now that the pump is primed, come up with a list that fits you. What matters is creating an atmosphere of loyalty to the kingdom of God as well as gratitude for what he's already done.

FROM FATHER TO SON

1. Find a "teachable time"—preferably when your son isn't in trouble—to share with him when you failed or were hurting when you were his age. Talk about how you felt when you let others down or were embarrassed to the point of shame.

2. Make a list of how you see your son—personality, strengths, gifts, talents—that come from the inside of him. Ask him to make his own list, and then compare and discuss your lists. Ask him to describe the differences between those times when he feels pressured by life and when he feels the way he is living comes directly from the inside.

3. Look for an opportunity to get your son talking about some memories he carries with him about your relationship. As you reminisce, ask if he remembers a time when

he felt you were a source of pressure for him to look or act a certain way that didn't feel like him. Ask for his forgiveness where necessary.

4. Ask a friend or two of yours to write your son a letter of encouragement, especially focusing on who they see him to be.

5. Celebrate something that really matters to your son, even (or especially) if it doesn't seem that big a deal to anyone else. Go all out!

GO FOR IT!

Think of something your son is good at or enjoys, and find a way to use that to serve the family in a significant way. (For example, plan a weekend vacation or arrange for everyone to go to a concert in another town.)

FROM FATHER TO FATHER

1. Because this may be a tough chapter for a few men, spend some time talking about the idea of living from the inside out. What does it mean? Can you tell when you are living authentically from the center of who God created you to be and when you are acting out of external roles expected by others?

2. How and when do you see your sons' most authentic self sneak out? How and when are they most vulnerable to try to please or perform for others by living from the outside? What can you do to encourage the authentic self more often?

CHAPTER 7

GOAL #2:
TO LOVE AS JESUS LOVED

> Power, no matter how well-intentioned, tends to
> cause suffering. Love, being vulnerable, absorbs it. In
> a point of convergence on a hill called Calvary, God
> renounced the one for the sake of the other.
>
> —PHILIP YANCEY

WHEN OUR SON ROB TURNED TEN, HE DID SOMETHING STRANGE. We still can't quite figure it out—it seemed so odd. But it helped us to understand this kid's heart a little bit more clearly.

Rob had received nearly 150 dollars for his birthday (not a normal practice in our family, but that's another story). The next day he and his six-year-old little sister, Katie, were hanging out in the neighborhood pet store waiting for Dee to finish some shopping. As they were looking at the birds, Katie fell head-over-heels for a love-bird that was for sale. The 105-dollar price tag, plus the cost of a cage and supplies, didn't dampen her enthusiasm; she just knew she had to have that bird. When Dee came into the store to get the kids and saw Robbie standing in line with an armload of merchandise, he simply stated matter-of-factly, "I'm getting Katie a bird." And so he did— bird, cage, food, the works. One minute he had 150 dollars in cash in his wallet, the next minute he was helping her out to the car with Petey, the newest member of the family.

It happened so quickly that Dee was more stunned than anything else. When they got home and introduced Chap (then thirteen) and me to the bird, we couldn't believe the story. We were blown away that Robbie would have shot all of his money . . . on a bird! But he quickly pointed out that he didn't spend *any* of his money on a bird; he had spent his money on his sister. To this day, he has never questioned whether his decision or his desire to take what was his and offer it as a gift to his sister was appropriate. To him, it was simply what he thought he "was supposed" to do.

This story has been cemented into our family lore, with great fondness and awe. Rob, in his own gentle but rather unorthodox way, taught all of us what it means to love and to live out of a commitment to regular, abandoned sacrifice for others. I wish I could take credit for being the instrument God used to teach this to my son, but at ten, he proved that in this area he's far ahead of me. Maybe you're thinking that at his age, he didn't completely understand what he was doing. But that's precisely the point. Out of the wonder of his childlikeness, Rob reminded our family that nothing we have is truly ours and that we are just temporary distributors of God's resources so that we may bless others.

Whenever we tell this story, we realize that Rob helped draw us closer to Jesus than a year's worth of Sunday school lessons. It was real. It was authentic. It was sacrificial. Rob taught us what it means to love, and to love sacrificially.

THE (ALMOST) UNTEACHABLE GOAL: TO LOVE SACRIFICIALLY

FEW THINGS ARE MORE IMPORTANT THAN TO HELP YOUR SON SEE life as a way to sacrificially shower others with extravagant love. This is maybe the grandest piece of the grand adventure of faith: we get to blow others away with overwhelming kindness and generosity. Following Jesus simply means this: We're invited into a life that has one ultimate purpose—being conduits of God's grace and kindness.

Jesus personified this conviction as he fleshed out his controversial passion for the best of others. He did and said things—all in the name of love—that didn't fit the norms or expectations of his world. He risked social scandal when he sat down for a conversation with a "wild woman" in Samaria (see John 4). He partied with the perceived morally decadent of his day, even to the point where he was called "a glutton and a drunkard, a friend of tax collectors [basically viewed as treasonous leeches] and 'sinners'" (Matthew 11:19).

The religious leaders of his day couldn't see how Jesus' willingness to be with the "sick" (Matthew 9:12) was an act of sacrificial care and love. They only criticized him. They were far more concerned with his relationship and association with the "right" people than they were with his willingness to love others. Love may have been important (and it's clear that the Pharisees believed this as well), but it was a secondary consideration following convention and decorum.

The point is that Jesus never once allowed cultural convention or the expectations of others—even religious custom or bias—to sway him from fresh, real, and abandoned love for people. This kind of love and care is simply the essence of Christ's message: Life is about loving others—even if and when it is costly—and making their lives as wonderful and meaningful as possible. There's no other message. We are lovers, plain and simple.

Jesus not only lived this way, he also taught that there's no other way to live. His single most focused command was the command to love. On the night before his death on the cross, Jesus gathered his friends and charged them to concentrate on nothing else:

"A new command I give you: Love one another.
As I have loved you, so you must love one
another. By this all men will know that you are

my disciples, if you love one another."
(John 13:34-35)

That same night, he repeated this command:

"My command is this: Love each other as I have
loved you." (John 15:12)

And again a few verses later:

"This is my command: Love each other."
(John 15:17)

However, although this is perhaps the most straightforward directive Jesus ever gave, the church seems to be
uncomfortable with the implications of his command. To
love as he loved? To love even when it's costly, makes no
sense, or when others see it as foolish?

"This is my command: Love each other."

WHAT DOES IT MEAN TO LOVE?

EARLIER I SAID ONE OF THE KEY MARKS OF A DISCIPLE IS TO BE A
lover. But in a world where everyone watches out for himself, helping your son to grow and develop as a lover-
disciple is a daunting challenge. Your son needs all the
help he can get to understand, recognize, and ultimately
internalize this great truth. Especially during his adolescent
years, focus on self and on caring for and protecting his
own soul is an essential part of his daily regimen. In a
world that can often feel hostile—where friends turn on
you without warning, teachers and coaches unceasingly
demand conformity or consistent performance, and messages proclaim that drinking, drugs, and sexual adventures
are more promising than what you have been taught—it
can be hard for a young man to muster the resources to

think about anyone but himself. Survival is the name of the game during his adolescent years. Sacrifice and extravagant devotion to an abandoned life of love isn't even on the adolescent radar screen.

But you can't ignore the fact that the central teaching of Christian faith, and the only command that Jesus himself made clear, is this: A disciple loves, and loves well.

TO LOVE IS TO LIVE IN SACRIFICIAL RELATIONSHIPS

FOR MOST PEOPLE I KNOW, SACRIFICE ISN'T THE FIRST WORD THEY'D use to describe their faith. It seems that phrases like "sacrificial living" have evaporated out of our Christian dictionary. Sure, we're called to love, but to truly sacrifice? Here's where you can be a powerful teacher for your son—to teach him what it means to love sacrificially.

It's often helpful to go back and see how a word came into being in the first place. Many of us have the idea that sacrifice is something negative and that we should avoid it. It's a word that seems to dwell more on the pain of the giver than on the blessing offered the receiver. Originally, however, sacrifice (Latin, *sacrificium)* described a noble action that, when offered as a gift, takes on extraordinary meaning and power. The word comes from two Latin words meaning literally "to make sacred" *(facere, sacer),* or to take something relatively ordinary and transform it into a sacred or holy item or activity. Taken this way, sacrificial love is extraordinary because it's an act of love. And by its focus on the beloved, it's literally made sacred. This means that you're called to help your son see that anything he offers to others isn't really about him at all; rather, it's about the power the act of love has for the person he's loving.

When I give my money or time or attention to another, it's not about what I give; it's about what God does with my offering. Sacrificial love is what Jesus meant when he said, "Greater love has no one than this, that he lay down his life for his friends" (John 15:13).

According to the Bible, as a follower of Christ your son

is invited into this kind of sacrificial living as his central calling in life. There isn't now—and never will be—a higher calling for your son; he's designed to be an instrument of God's overflowing and rich blessing to others. He's been set free to be used by God to set others free, thus offering himself as one of many "living sacrifices, holy and pleasing to God" (Romans 12:1).

Like Robbie and his birthday money, everything your son is and everything he has is an acceptable and qualified resource for God's blessing to others. This is what his faith ultimately means. His focus on sacrifice isn't an invitation to be "spiritual"; rather, it's a call to see that everything your son holds dear is handed over to God in a way that directly impacts other people's lives. To live as a disciple of Jesus Christ means that your son learns to see that he is called to be a compassionate and extravagant lover who doesn't seek his own but instead expresses his faith by how he cares for others sacrificially. His entire faith can be boiled down to this single focused calling: to love others with an abandoned and sacrificial passion.

What does this mean practically? Do I teach my son that it's more important to help others to succeed even if it costs him? Or to take responsibility for his lying or cheating whether he's been found out or not? Or to be willing to take a hit for someone who can't defend himself? Or to spend his money buying a bird for his little sister?

As harsh as these seem to our human ears, that's precisely what sacrificial love means. It's hard. It's radical. It makes no sense. Yet Jesus taught and clearly modeled this way of living. He took the sacrificial route, and he calls you to teach your son to follow him.

THE GOAL OF SACRIFICE: LETTING GO OF SELF

JESUS DESCRIBES THIS LIFESTYLE IN THE BEATITUDES (SEE MATTHEW 5:3-12), which represent exactly the spirit of this ideal. Jesus' call to be meek, merciful, pure in heart, a peacemaker, and willing to be persecuted for what is good and right exemplifies exactly what it means to live out a commitment of sacrificial love.

As you help your son to see life as a journey of love, remember that true change and authentic transformation only come through the power of the Holy Spirit. The inner strength he needs to live out the Beatitudes is only possible when God has been building himself into the fabric of your son's soul. You can't program or train this. As much as I'd like to give you a few simple steps to build this strength into your son, it really comes down to the mysterious relationship and interaction between your son and God's Spirit.

I can offer you hope—a lot of it—because this power, the grace that transforms our attitudes and perspectives, is a free gift to anyone who responds to God's call and who seeks "first his kingdom and his righteousness" (Matthew 6:33). You can be sure God wants your son to develop into a man who knows and loves him and who lives this out in his everyday relationships. And because of this, you can rest assured that as your son grows in his relationship with Jesus Christ, the Beatitudes will become a natural product of his life. As he responds to the calling to live as a committed man of faith, you can know that he'll grow in his ability to see loving others as his first and only commitment on earth. God himself will be prompting this response, and the interaction between the Spirit's calling and your son's response will create the growth toward maturity in love. This is what the apostle Paul meant in these passages:

> The entire law is summed up in a single command: "Love your neighbor as yourself."
> (Galatians 5:14)

> Do nothing out of selfish ambition or vain conceit, but in humility consider others better than yourselves. Each of you should look not only to your own interests, but also to the interests of

others. Your attitude should be the same as that
of Christ Jesus. (Philippians 2:3-5)

This is the raw stuff of discipling our sons. If we don't
model and teach our boys how to yield to God's nudge
toward sacrificial relationships, then having a daily prayer
time, reading Christian books, memorizing Scripture, listening to Christian music, and even practicing more formal
classical disciplines like fasting and meditation will have
very little effect. Spiritual disciplines and activities are vital
and obviously have their place. They encourage us to slow
down long enough to let God speak into our souls. But
they aren't a substitute for the sacrificial life God has called
us to live.

There are three ways your son can be prepared for the
Spirit's work in his life. The first two you can encourage
and foster. The third—internalizing the sacrificial life—is
between your son and his God.

#1—Understanding the Sacrificial Life

To help your son understand what sacrificial living and loving is, create a category, a kind of computer file folder, in
his worldview. You want to create a space reserved for the
idea of sacrificial living. In today's society, we all have so
much information to process. The primacy of our faith
demands that we proactively create the kind of setting
where our sons can make lifelong emotional and spiritual
deposits. Your son won't become a sacrificial, loving servant overnight, but your role is to make room for this idea
in his head and heart.

Here are some ideas to make this happen with your
son (while some may seem obvious or repetitive, it is
amazing how easy it is to forget the obvious in our daily
lives):

* Model a lifestyle of sacrifice and commitment that
  has the best of others in mind, even when it's
  costly.

- Consistently talk about love as the obvious and notable outcome of authentic faith. As Paul wrote, "The grace of our Lord was poured out on me abundantly, along with the faith and love that are in Christ Jesus" (1 Timothy 1:14).
- Whenever someone makes a clear choice (an individual, group, or institution) *not* to love sacrificially, point it out. Let your son struggle with the issues that bother you.
- Television, films, songs, and many other sources communicate to your son how he should think about love and sacrifice. This occurs in something as mundane as the scene in *It's a Wonderful Life* where the entire town donates their own money to save the Savings and Loan, or as a sacrifice bunt in baseball. When possible, use these moments to discuss the ideas of sacrifice and love with your son.
- Look and listen for perceived or real "gray areas" that both you and your son need to think through and consider theologically. Invite him to let you know when and where he's touched by something from the world, and discuss with him how this fits with God's calling on his life to sacrificial, abandoned love.

#2—Recognizing the Sacrificial Life

This stage of leading your son is the bridge between a cognitive understanding (head knowledge) of what sacrificial loving is and the laboratory to learn how to recognize it when it occurs. You won't (and shouldn't) be able to force your son to recognize this kind of extravagant loving. But you can watch and listen for clues that he's beginning to see for himself that sacrificial loving is all that really matters.

Here are a few ideas to help your son grow in recognizing God's grace at work:

- Through role-play or in a more straightforward discussion, ask your son to define the idea of sacrificial living for someone else.
- As you move through the years, look for times when your son articulates an encounter with the antithesis of sacrificial love—everything from blatant arrogance and inappropriate ego assertion to just plain selfishness. Do your best to engage your son in conversation about what he has witnessed. Beware not to push too hard. It's more important that you watch and listen carefully as your son seeks to discover for himself what it means to become a sacrificial lover.
- Point out to your son whenever you hear or see him displaying even the tiniest glimmer of sacrificial or extravagant love.

#3—Internalizing the Sacrificial Life

When Rob bought Katie that bird, it was such an act of pure and innocent love that it clearly came from the inside out. We can't hope to *create* inside our sons that kind of authentic love. Real love—the kind Jesus modeled, taught, and calls us to—comes from the deepest part of a person's soul. As your son yields more and more of his life to Jesus as Lord, as he embraces the truth that God's voice constantly encourages him toward sacrificial love, and as he lets go of what the world says a "real man" is like and allows the Scriptures to form his commitment to "lay his life down" for the good of others, he'll show you the unique way God can use him as a beacon of light and compassion.

Sacrificial love can be neither legislated nor coerced, for as soon as it becomes a duty, it ceases to be sacred. Your role is to consistently remind your son that faith only makes sense when he allows God's heart to transform his and that Jesus knew what he was talking about when he said, "Whoever wants to save his life will lose it, but whoever loses his life for me will save it" (Luke 9:24).

FROM FATHER TO SON

1. When the situation is right, confess to your son when you become aware of times in your life that don't represent the most loving response. Ask him to pray for you.

2. After you've created a steady stream of examples of when you have been willing to confess and grow with your own weaknesses in this area, invite him to consider when he may have been less than loving in an attitude, comment, or response. Pray for each other.

3. Invite your son to hold you accountable if he sees you harboring a spirit of contention or arrogance. Your attitude may not even be overt, but give him permission to sit down with you and point out what he sees. (You'll never find a better way to teach him to be humble and receive correction as he grows up.)

4. Write him a note when you see even the slightest growth in sacrificial love, even if only in his attitude. (The actions will follow eventually.)

GO FOR IT!

Do something together that enables you to see and interact with people who are broken, oppressed, or poor. Arrange for your whole family to learn sign language, or volunteer monthly to drive a disabled person to church or school, or include shut-ins in your Thanksgiving or Christmas celebrations. Just do something together that shows your son how to consider a sacrificial option as a daily discipline of mature faith.

FROM FATHER TO FATHER

1. What does the concept of "sacrifice" mean to you? When have you personally seen or experienced sacrificial love in action?

2. Who's the most sacrificial "lover" in your family (even extended family)? Talk about the characteristics or marks

that cause you to single out this person. What makes some people more sacrificial than others in the way they live their lives? How can dads instill these qualities in their sons?

3. Where have your sons displayed sacrificial love? Share ideas about how to encourage your sons to see the joy of sacrifice for the good of others.

CHAPTER 8

GOAL #3:
TO SEE LIFE AS A JOURNEY HOMEWARD

I want to know one thing—the way to heaven; how to land safe on that happy shore. God himself has condescended to teach the way; for this very end he came from heaven.

—JOHN WESLEY

I HAVE A CLOSE FRIEND NAMED RALPH WHO, DURING ANY DISCUS-sion or dreaming session, is notorious for bringing people back to earth by asking the question, "What's the goal?" With a few others, Dee and I have been wading around in some of the more nebulous language of contemporary spirituality, regularly using words like "journey" and "soul." Ralph has taken on the role of keeping our feet on the ground by repeating his standard query. He forces our group to main-tain some semblance of real direction and purpose in our quest for meaningful Christianity in a changing world.

Whenever we get to this point, we end up acknowl-edging that when we sift out all the rhetoric, the ultimate goal in life is very concrete: we're called to live as men and women on the road home to heaven. God has his people on a quest toward eternity. Reaching home is the goal of our faith, and this truth may just be the simplest descrip-tion of the Christian journey.

When was the last time you talked to your son—or, for that matter, to anyone—about heaven? If you're like most guys, not in a long, long time. This topic probably hasn't come into your conversations since the hamster died or an episode of *The Simpsons* took a shot at it. We hear about it in popular culture occasionally when someone writes a song (like Eric Clapton's *Tears in Heaven*) or if it's a theme on television (as in episodes of *Touched by an Angel*). But the actual place—the lifelong goal of our faith—is so rarely discussed today. Maybe we're somehow embarrassed by the idea of heaven. Or at least we're not sure what to think about heaven. For many contemporary Christians, heaven just doesn't seem to be on the radar screen. But when you look at the Scriptures, you know it should be.

The fact that we seldom talk about heaven begs this question: How much emphasis should we give the idea of heaven as we lead our boys on their faith journeys? Does seeing heaven as his real home matter that much in a world where he'll have to muster all his resources simply to survive as a sacrificially devoted man of God? The answer, if we're to understand faith as a response to God's plan as revealed in Scripture, is a resounding *of course it matters!* Heaven is core to your son's faith because it's where he'll reside with the Lord for all eternity. It's the place he was created to live in, in intimate relationship with God and the saints. So asking what heaven is like *does* matter. By asking this question, your son will begin to look at what he's preparing for, living for, and moving toward.

This life is filled with heartache, confusion, and pain. You'll watch your son experience disappointment, failure, and insecurity. You'll watch as he learns what it means to be beaten down and discouraged. Sometimes the choices he makes will result in these disappointments. Sometimes life's struggles will cause him to become acutely aware of how sinful and dark the world really is. The biblical prescription for the trials and heartache of this world is to keep our eyes fixed on our heavenly home. Your son's best shot for growing as a man of God is to keep his eyes fixed on his calling heavenward, knowing that life is a journey into the embrace of the God who loves him.

HEAVEN – THE GOAL OF OUR JOURNEY

THE NIGHT BEFORE JESUS WAS CRUCIFIED, HE SPENT HOURS WITH his best friends in a room, sharing a meal and offering them specific encouragement and instructions. Known as the Upper Room Discourse, the last few chapters of John's gospel offer us a window into Jesus' most pointed teaching in the Bible. Throughout his ministry he talked about heaven, but in light of the solemn setting of that night, his words take the issue of the homeward goal of our journey to new heights. On this last night with his disciples before he was put to death, notice how Jesus' words and prayer compare our place in the earthly world to the journey he calls us to:

> "If you belonged to the world, it would love you as its own. As it is, you do not belong to the world, but I have chosen you out of the world. That is why the world hates you. . . .
>
> "I have given them your word and the world has hated them, for they are not of the world any more than I am of the world. My prayer is not that you take them out of the world but that you protect them from the evil one. They are not of the world, even as I am not of it. Sanctify them by the truth; your word is truth. As you sent me into the world, I have sent them into the world." (John 15:19; 17:14-18)

As a disciple of Jesus Christ, your son does not and will not ever belong to the world. God has "chosen" him "out of the world." God has literally *lifted* your son out of one world and placed him in a new world, complete with a new identity and a new home. Your son doesn't really belong here anymore; he's been lifted into a new reality with a new address. Because of what Christ has done for him, he no longer belongs to this world, this place, or this time. His life on earth is simply his journey home.

Notice Jesus' prayer for both you and your son: "My prayer is not that you take them out of the world but that you protect them from the evil one." Even though this life is not home, God in his perfect and life-fulfilling plan chooses to leave us here for a season. Your son is essentially on loan to this world, even though it's not the world he belongs to. And Jesus reminds him that as he moves through life, he'll be harassed by the evil one along the way. God understands this and is well aware that many voices will seek to draw your son away from this focus on the journey homeward. The Great Adversary, other people, and even culture itself will barrage your son (and you) with the message that the world is his only safe place and that he doesn't need to look further for his true home.

Jesus' prayer shows that this is one of the most important battles for the soul of your son. The Father knows and loves your boy and invites him into that place he was created to experience and enjoy forever. Heaven is the only true home and the only sure safe place he'll ever find. We need to make this truth a significant focus as we lead our boys in their life of faith.

LIVING WITH HEAVEN AS THE GOAL

THERE ARE THREE ELEMENTS TO BUILDING A SENSE OF THE HOME-ward journey in the life of your son. First, he must come to the point where he recognizes this as a fact. Biblically, it is not an option. Our home is simply not here. Instead, home is in relationship with God beyond the confines of the time and space we now know. Second, he must see that heaven, as the pinnacle of his faith journey, is an attractive and desirable goal. And third, because heaven is best understood and even most often described in terms of relationships (because that's something we can grab hold of), he needs to come to see that those in the body of Christ are his true brothers and sisters, his real family. These three facets of the heavenward journey aren't sequential or separate. They're essentially three different angles of the same truth: heaven is our home, it is attractive, and with it comes a new family.

Angle #1—Recognize that Heaven Is Home

For your boy to grow as a mature and set-free follower of Jesus Christ, he needs to be convinced that God has lifted and chosen him out of the power, needs, and enticements of this world and set him on the road toward home. God has created your son with a longing for heaven, whether or not he recognizes it, and that thirst is only quenched as he allows God's Spirit to draw him close. Like most, he's probably not conscious of this longing; many people go through life like the lead character in the movie *As Good As It Gets*, thinking this world is all there is and we had better make the most of it. But God has built into your son the driving desire to spend eternity with his heavenly Father and to live in his home. Your son's dreams, his ambition, and his life's fulfillment are all waiting to be discovered and experienced as he comes to see that he has a new home called heaven.

Holding fast to this perspective will empower your son to live a life true to his homeward calling. This awareness can lift him above the oppression and suffocation of his earthly life and enable him to withstand and endure the sorrows and disappointments that are a natural part of this fallen world. Having this perspective on our earthly life is a consistent theme throughout Scripture. As James put it: "Consider it pure joy, my brothers, whenever you face trials of many kinds, because you know that the testing of your faith develops perseverance. Perseverance must finish its work so that you may be mature and complete, not lacking anything" (James 1:2-4).

Our side of the "faith formula" is to hang in there—to persevere, holding tight to the truth we've been given. When James talked about trials, he referred to those circumstances in life that can shake our trust in God as safe and good. The idea of considering as "pure joy" things that cause us to hurt and fear can seem like a superficial, simplistic, and almost ridiculous antidote to the dark and lonely realities of life in this world. But teaching your son to do what he can to emotionally and intellectually (with his heart and mind) trust his God and to remember his true home will produce in him the depth of determined faith (perseverance) that results in maturity. Living a life true to our eternal home gives us the ability to persevere. As your boy builds upon his heavenward focus and perspective, the resulting perseverance will work in your son to produce what you've always longed for—a young man who has become "mature and complete, not lacking anything" (James 1:4).

When I was in graduate school, a couple took me under their wing, almost like second parents. Burt took me to Dodger games, Joy did my laundry, and I used the key to their house to nab all the Pepsi I could sneak into my car (at their invitation). As a successful general manager for a major department store in town, Burt constantly challenged me about my schoolwork, my grades, and the business side of my ministerial education. Joy's job was to keep me humble and dating the "right kind of girls." But they talked to me about Jesus and flamed my passion for helping teenagers to come to know him. Burt and Joy were on our local Young Life board, and I remember talking with them many times about God's purposes in our community, my calling as his servant, and our hope and true joy being found in Christ. They didn't use the word "heaven" to describe this faith, per se, but they pointed me in that direction. They were models who kept me focused on my true home. Their gentle leadership was a constant reminder of the journey toward heaven, and they helped to shape me into the man I am today.

Angle #2—See that Heaven Is Attractive
What's heaven really like?

When my middle son, Rob, was around six or seven years old, this is exactly the kind of question he would pepper me with on a daily basis. I especially remember one conversation when he wouldn't accept my stock answer and let go of it.

"Dad, I mean . . . is it *fun?*"

"What do you mean by 'fun'?"

"You know what I mean, Dad. Are there computer games, football on TV, and vacations? You know, fun!"

How do *you* deal with that kind of question? As you attempt to pass on a vibrant, authentic faith to your son, it's a very important question. So, what would you say? What do you think—what's heaven like?

As I've played with this over the past decade or so since Rob's inquiry, here are a few scenarios I've somehow picked up along the way:

- Heaven is a perpetual worship service where the faithful gather and listen to angels sing and apostles preach, and Jesus comes on near the end as the headliner. The Father sits onstage with a knowing look and a smiling presence, and the Holy Spirit darts around the assembly prompting audience participation.
- Heaven is a place of eternal rest where we don't have to attend meetings, return phone calls or e-mails, or fulfill any obligations. We're invited—in fact, systemically "encouraged"—to sit back and soak in the heavenly life.
- Heaven is a huge, passionate concert where everyone comes onstage and angels teach choruses to masses of adoring "fans" who sing, dance, clap their hands, and generally whoop it up.
- Heaven is simply standing around doing a few things, running a few errands, but none of it really matters much—kind of like an ongoing, loving *The Truman Show.*

I know—what a foolish waste of time! How flippant can I get? After all, the kingdom of heaven is the final destination of our faith, where the streets are paved with gold. Yes, it might be important to help my son to recognize that his true home is in heaven, but to think about it in these kinds of ways seems simplistic at best. Frankly, I think we *must* sometimes toy with exaggeration to dissect and deconstruct the neat, tidy categories of faith that hold little or no meaning for postmodern young people. The concept of heaven is central to the historic Christian faith. Yet it remains a rather fuzzy, religiously influenced idea that contemporary believers really don't think they need to spend a great deal of time on. In the minds of most honest Christians, heaven matters only in theory; it has very little impact on the day-to-day existence of Jesus' followers. But Jesus talked a lot about heaven, and on the night before he died he prayed that his followers would keep that perspective.

Let's start with a simple, clean fact: heaven *is* attractive. Actually, heaven is so far beyond attractive that we don't even have a word for it. In the Old Testament the Hebrew word for heaven (or "heavens"), *shamayim,* is used 420 times to describe God's home, but nowhere is it used to imply that this place is also for the rest of God's people. Heaven was just seen as too majestic, too holy for us mortal humans. That all changed with the arrival of Jesus.

In the New Testament, Jesus blew open the doors to heaven. He brought the royal reign of God to those he had created and called, and this kingdom reign extends beyond time and culminates in entrance into heaven. Jesus taught that the kingdom is both a current reality and a future promise, and it crescendos with the community of God's people celebrating eternal life together in perfect love and unimaginable joy for all eternity— *in heaven!* Jesus always describes heaven as the natural and desirable result of faith. People in Jesus' day knew that heaven was the absolute fulfillment of every human longing and desire, and to be invited was the greatest gift a person could ever be offered.

But what is heaven *like?*

That remains a tough question for dads of the new millennium, for we (and our sons) think more in terms of what we will do there than about the place itself. Jesus loved to talk about heaven, but he usually did it using parables and stories that described the idea or feel of heaven more than the schematic layout and daily schedule. In two of his more pointed parables, the great treasure (see Matthew 13:44) and the pearl of great price (see Matthew 13:45-46), Jesus said that whatever heaven is like, it brings such joy that a man would go and sell "all he had" to obtain it. Jesus assumes we know that heaven is so wonderful, so exciting, and so inviting that all who truly know what is waiting for them will surely come to him.

The next time you talk with your son about heaven and he either balks or presses you on what it's "like," play Socrates with him by asking questions in return. If I were with Rob back at seven years old again, here's how I would try to steer that conversation:

"Dad, what's heaven like?"

"Rob, what's the most important thing in your life?"

"Ummm . . . Abby" (his dog).

"Heaven will be so much more valuable to you than even Abby."

"But what is there to do in heaven?"

"Rob, of anything you can imagine, what's your favorite thing to do?"

"Meeting John Elway, Dad!" (I'd taken his brother a few weeks before to meet John Elway, something that I have yet to live down.)

"Rob, as great as John Elway is, heaven will be so much more exciting than even meeting John Elway."

"Dad, what are we going to do in heaven?"

"What is the greatest thing you have ever done?"

"Going to a Broncos game and going fishing on the boat with Grandpa."

"Rob, it's better than that . . . way better!"

This may sound trite and superficial, but a lifetime of conversations like this—especially when seasoned with a gleam in your eye and your own inner sense of anticipation—will plant the seeds of the eternal in your son. This is the "outside" work of training we dads are called to. At the same time, you need to trust that the Spirit is whispering this same truth in the inner core of your son's heart.

After all, God is the one who is calling your boy to an intimate relationship for eternity. Don't worry, Dad. God is calling him home. Here are Jesus' words for your son as well as for the disciples on the night before he died: "In my Father's house are many rooms; if it were not so, I would have told you. I am going there to prepare a place for you. And if I go and prepare a place for you, I will come back and take you to be with me that you also may be where I am" (John 14:2-3).

Your son needs to realize that the place Jesus is preparing for him will be so much greater, so much bigger, and so much more satisfying than anything he has experienced or ever will experience here on earth. Heaven is attractive!

Angle #3—See that Heaven Is Being with Your Eternal Family

As your son's father, you'll impact his life at least as much as anyone else, for good and for bad. More than anyone else he encounters, your family will make the boldest mark on his soul and behavior. But your son also needs others so he can become the person God created him to be. His immediate family isn't enough, and God never intended it to be enough.

One day, Jesus' mother and brothers were concerned that he was "out of his mind" (Mark 3:21) and showed up to take him home. Not understanding his message and method, they had come to try to talk some sense into him. When told they were outside wanting to see him, Jesus replied, "Who is my mother, and who are my brothers?" Then, "pointing to his disciples, he said, 'Here are my mother and my brothers. For whoever does the will of my Father in heaven is my brother and sister and mother'" (Matthew 12:48-50). Jesus wanted his followers to know that in God's kingdom, all followers of Jesus belong to each other just as much as biological family members belong to each other. Perhaps this familial bond is intended to be even tighter than blood.

To help your son see and appreciate this, the relationships your family models throughout his childhood and adolescence will set the stage for the quality and kind of relationships he'll experience and cling to for the rest of his life. Does he see your adult Christian friends as part of his family? Do you talk about and treat others as nearly as important as your nuclear family? If so, this will be the best gift you can give to your son. Heaven is primarily a *relational* home, where those we love and connect to form the intimacy of the eternal community.

Most parents want to make their earthly home a safe haven for all kinds of kids. Of course, that's a positive thing because it sends the message to your children that you're trustworthy and safe. But in the long run, the more important issue is how they experience your friends and your relationships. If you connect with other believers in family-like ways, and your son is drawn into these relationships, he'll grow up knowing that he's part of something far bigger than his family. He'll get a taste of what it means to live life in exile while on a journey home together. And the truth of what it means to live in God's family will become an integral part of who he is and who he becomes.

This idea is far more organic than programmatic. The essence of building into your son an understanding of and appreciation for the body of Christ as his true eternal family is primarily found in how your family lives in relationship to others. If you're a family committed to opening up your lives to others in intimate community and if you recognize that as followers of Christ you need to hold the boundaries of the nuclear family loosely, you'll provide the kind of environment where your son will pick up this same conviction.

Here are some of the ways Dee and I have gone about this in our twenty-one years of marriage:

- For nearly our entire married life we have been involved in some form of small-group community. The adults in these groups have also seen themselves as responsible for and connected to our kids (and us to theirs). We've all watched—and even helped—our friends' kids grow up. When someone

needed encouragement or was celebrating a special
event, we've all been there for each other (as much
as we could). When the adults gathered and connected, we've intentionally included our kids in
those relationships.

- During holidays and at other times, we've brought
  people into our home as members of the family.
  Whether a young woman needing a quiet place for
  a few weeks to prepare for her wedding, a young
  man needing to be loved by a family at Christmas,
  or a family new to the area needing friends, we've
  worked hard to maintain the balance between the
  needs of our own family and the desire to walk out
  our commitment to live as the body of Christ.

- Our goal has been to create a home atmosphere
  where people—even strangers—feel welcome
  when they come over. We've always wanted the
  kind of house where kids feel safe and comfortable. We've also sought to maintain a style of
  hospitality where, even when it's somewhat incon-
  venient for us, people feel they can enter our
  home and our lives.

- Perhaps the most significant strategy we've had is to
  encourage our friends to also be our kids' friends.
  Jeff and Nancy Ward, for example, have known our
  sons well since they were born. Our kids honestly
  believe the Wards are part of our family. Now that
  their kids are getting older, our sons are taking
  ownership in them, even spiritually. Just last week
  we overheard Rob talking to Trent, the Ward's
  eight-year-old, about his faith and asking Trent
  questions about his life. When one of our boys
  was running for an office in junior high, Mike
  Yaconelli—author, international speaker, and leader
  of a large youth ministry—spent an hour helping
  him to write his nomination speech. Our son didn't
  win, but he'll always love Mike for the time and
  focused commitment.

This is rubbing off on our sons, and we couldn't be more grateful for the dozens of close friends who've poured into their lives. This has been a more powerful witness to the family of God than we ever could have imagined.

HEADING HOME

JUST LIKE CHRISTMAS SPECIALS SELLING THE IDEA THAT COMING home is the point of Christmas, for those of us who've been "seized by a great affection" (to quote Brennan Manning), there's a home we're traveling toward. It took Oz's Dorothy several costume changes and plot twists to finally recognize "there's no place like home." We seem to operate as though earthly life is the home we were created for. Sure, heaven will be good (somehow). But our primary focus is on creating the best home we can here.

Yet the gospel's radical message is that this life is not now, nor could it ever be, home. Our true home is in heaven, and every step of the journey we take brings us closer to experiencing the Great Homecoming. We have a map, and we have a destination. As your son walks with Christ, where is he headed? He is going home!

FROM FATHER TO SON

1. Make note of a time or situation when your son is extraordinarily happy. Later, refer back to that event or experience and connect it to heaven. Let him know that these types of feelings, and so many others in life, are little gifts—tiny glimpses of what's in store for us in heaven.

2. Watch for some common reference to heaven or heavenly things (like angels) in a song, movie, or TV show. Talk with your son about heaven and the journey home. Help him to look for reminders that he's actually headed toward his true home. Help him to see it as fantastic beyond his wildest imagination.

3. Go through some of Jesus' parables on heaven with your son. Work together to help to him connect the truth God offers to his everyday life.

GO FOR IT!

Decide as a family what people or families you want to get closer to. Plan some specific steps to consider ways to create an eternal community on earth. Make sure you ground this in the idea of God's heavenly family as you proceed.

FROM FATHER TO FATHER

1. Obviously, the content of this chapter must begin with you as fathers looking at these issues separate and apart from your sons. What do *you* think of when it comes to heaven as the end destination of your faith? Is it supremely desirable or something less? As honestly as you can, describe your feelings and thoughts with each other.

2. If you've had conversations with your sons about heaven, how have they gone? If you haven't, talk about why. Discuss how difficult it may be for you to talk with your sons about heaven and an intimate relationship with God and his family for eternity.

3. Discuss who the people are that comprise your lifelong, intimate, Christ-centered spiritual community. Are you currently satisfied with this list or the length of it? What would it mean to be more intentional about these kinds of relationships?

4. Talk to each other about your sons — their strengths, dreams, ambitions, and temperaments. Pray together for adults to come alongside each of the boys represented in your group. Consider how you could be friends to each other's sons.

CHAPTER 9

GOAL #4:
TO SEE LIFE AS A GRAND ADVENTURE

In the beginning of His ministry, Jesus was continually bumping into fishermen, tax collectors, and political activists and asking them to follow Him. Astonishingly, these men abandoned their careers, their families, and their futures to follow Jesus. All because this Jesus said, "Follow Me." Why? Why would these men give up all they knew to follow Jesus into what they didn't know? Because somehow these men *knew* that life with Jesus is the life they had been seeking unsuccessfully in the confines of safety and caution. They *knew* life's greatest adventure was waiting just beyond the limits of carefulness. They *knew* where the music was coming from.

—MIKE YACONELLI

"THAT'S A LIE!"

I'd been on a roll during my first year of teaching graduate ministry students. I was enthusiastic, passionate, and (I thought) engaging. How could a student interrupt me in such a rude way?

"Excuse me?"

"What you just said—about life being a grand adventure . . . that's a lie."

I was dumbfounded, and I found myself left uncharacteristically speechless. The entire class of thirty or so simply waited for him to go on. After a brief pause, this man in his early thirties began to describe how he believed we need to tell people the truth about being a Christian. "Life is anything but an adventure, even for Christians," he snarled. "It's hard, painful, and people are jerks."

After catching my breath, I pried out of him some of the experiences that tainted his perspective on life, even a life of faith. The gist of his disappointment revolved around his last two jobs, both in churches. He'd been fired from one and he'd recently resigned from the other due to "political maneuvering and compromise" of the pastoral staff in dealing with "powerful, arrogant people" in the congregation. He was more than cynical; he was nearly destroyed.

"Life is difficult" is how M. Scott Peck begins his classic book, *The Road Less Traveled*. Indeed, who could argue with that? Every father knows that the world he prepares his son for will mercilessly and relentlessly try to destroy his soul. And just because he grows up as a Christian does not mean he'll be protected from the heartache and struggles of living in a fallen, fragmented world. The Pollyannaish, non-biblical yet oft-stated Christian line "Come to Jesus, and he'll shield you from pain, calm your storms, and give you all the desires of your heart" simply doesn't cut it in the harsh reality of everyday life. A superficial reading of the Bible may seem to point to a gospel that heals all brokenness and promises daily sunshine. But an honest reading of the Bible and an evenly slightly mature perspective of faith affirm that God's love and mercy do not guarantee a life free from pain, discomfort, or suffering. In fact, the opposite is true: faith opens our eyes to wrong in the world, and therefore is often the cause of increased suffering and discomfort. Peck had it right. Life—even for the committed follower of Jesus Christ—is difficult.

This said, the gospel offers hope and a worldview for your son that penetrates far deeper than a promise of cosmetic solace and a guarantee of a worry-free middle-class lifestyle. The gospel offers truth. For your boy, the gospel presents an opportunity to discover and experience life itself, what Jesus called "life . . . to the full," or abundant life. (John 10:10). The gospel is Jesus' wild passion, enticing presence, penetrating dancing eyes, and nail-scarred hands outstretched, inviting your son to a whole new quality of life. God in creation and redemption has orchestrated the most audacious experience a human being could ever hope to have. This is the Grand Adventure of faith!

LIFE AS A GRAND ADVENTURE? GIVE ME A BREAK!

AS MY SON'S FATHER, I HAVE BOTH THE HONOR AND THE RESPONsibility to teach him what's important in life. My loudest words will be how I live my life. If I tell my son God is good and life is an adventure to be pursued, but I walk through the door after ten hours of work with a perpetual scowl on my face, do you think he'll really believe what I say? If I teach him God owns the cattle on a thousand hills, yet complain nonstop about our financial woes or allow our family to be tyrannized by consumption and debt, what lesson will he learn about the wonder of faith, hope, and love? If I memorize with him passages where God has invited us into his kingdom as "little children" who are called to live with an abandoned sense of purpose, but then live and act as if my world revolves around the here and now, how will he ultimately define his life of faith?

Whether the issue is choosing friends, performing on an athletic field, or getting decent grades, the stresses on today's adolescents are greater than ever before. Some argue that this generation of adolescents is more stressed out and pressured than any in recent history, maybe in history's entirety. Families are under greater strain just to stay connected; teachers demand more hours of homework than ever; coaches expect year-round, multi-day devotion from about the third grade on; and the general frantic pace of life keeps kids in constant motion. Their lives are clearly busier than in any previous generation. But, interestingly, in my experience, they tend to be less motivated, more easily discouraged and disengaged, and far more cynical than ever.

Today high school life is often described using words like "survival" instead of "fun" and "free." As your son grows up in this environment, he'll face the temptation to join the crowd that sees life—even the Christian life—as a treadmill of dullness instead of a grand adventure. This will be one of your most daunting challenges.

I'm convinced God is wildly, madly, passionately in love with your son. I believe that God has created him to dance the great dance of faith with abandon and reckless commitment to Jesus Christ. The Scriptures are clear on this point: when Jesus called men and women to himself he demanded focused and unreasonable commitment to him and his kingdom. In this world of college and career, car payments and mortgages, programs and committee meetings, we may have inadvertently broken God's heart. The gospel is God's invitation to come and be blessed. His call is to rest. He promises life experienced from a sense of freedom and fueled by passionate abandonment. The result is satisfying soul-rest. The journey is meant to be danced, not shuffled.

A few years ago a seventeen-year-old boy named Craig ran away from home and I ended up being the one to find him. He was a great athlete and a fair student, but his father wasn't pleased with his performance in either setting. His grades were slipping, and he was having a tough go on the court. The more he tried to do well, the worse his performance became. Yet his dad pushed him all the harder. I'd known this man, and in my observation he was fairly typical as a father. He loved his son and wanted the best for him, but couldn't stop himself from badgering and challenging his son to work hard and stay on top of his game. In his enthusiasm, he'd pushed Craig to the edge.

As this tall, muscular man-boy sat before me and cried, I began to get a glimpse of how much stress he was under. All he wanted was for his father to see how hard he was working to please him. But whenever Craig tried talking to his dad about his life, he felt his dad move into critique-and-control mode. Whenever they talked, it usually deteriorated to the point where Craig shut down and his father pressed on to make the singular point that Craig had heard his entire life: Craig had no idea what "real work" was like, and how important it is to live up to life's commitments and to "be a man."

Things never really turned around for them. Craig was crying out for encouragement, comfort, understanding, and room to develop as a man and explore the fullness of what life had to offer. Sure, he needed to be taught responsibility, but the boxes he had found himself in were killing him. His father couldn't see that the way he was attempting to lead Craig was actually controlling his son's life to the point of suffocating him. Today Craig is still dogged by the need to perform, and he and his father have virtually no relationship at all. Some adventure!

LIFE AS A GRAND ADVENTURE: "WHAT A RIDE!"

I HAVE A RATHER PASSIONATE FRIEND NAMED MIKE YACONELLI WHO actually believes life is designed and even can be lived as a wild adventure. In his writing—including *Dangerous Wonder*—and his speaking, he constantly pushes people to consider life from a new perspective. We all get bogged down in meetings and strategies, in rules and roles, in mortgages and credit limits. Mike's message is that life is meant to be lived.

He describes the faith journey as the world's most ominous roller coaster. At first, after being strapped into the security and safety of the "car" of faith, the ride begins with a short, gentle turn and a consistent uphill climb where the anticipation of the journey is calm and the view is magnificent. But, at the top of the hill, the first screams are heard as the cars begin their terrifying catapult into unknown twists and turns. At breakneck speed, the coaster goes up and down, taking hairpin turns and threatening to topple the occupants onto the pavement stories below. Being thrown side to side, smashing into the person next to you, glasses flying from your pocket, the video camera ending up somewhere in the parking lot—eventually the delicious torment ends and, as soon as the car comes to a stop and the safety bar (an obvious oxymoron) is lifted, you hear yourself scream, "Let's do it again!"

According to Mike, that's how God created life. When it comes to your son, of course, there will be moments of joyful exhilaration and times when God's mercy is evident. But there will also be times in your boy's life that are filled with fear. When God seems distant, your son will wonder what is happening to him. He'll face questions and nightmares, smiles and songs, wailing and weeping, and even significant bumping into those around him. But if he stays the course and lives as an authentic, committed believer, when all is said and done—when he takes his last breath and the ride rolls to a stop—he'll be able to stare up into heaven with a joy that few can know and exclaim, "What . . . a . . . ride!"

For your son to see life this way means a whole new level of trust in the Designer. Most of us have lived in a T.G.I.F. society for so long we can't imagine an existence where living in the *now* is God's plan for the journey. What matters to us is our weekends, vacations, and holidays. Yet when they're finally upon us, we find ourselves secretly disappointed that they don't live up to the hype of our unspoken expectations. We have a hard time finding fulfillment in day-to-day living. When we arrive at the moment we've been anticipating, we intuitively recognize that we've missed something along the way.

That is because God created us and set us free to find life in the journey itself. The joy and power we experience depends on how we view the ride—either it's a directionless, pointless drudgery of pain, loneliness, and fear, or it's an exhilarating catapult over the edge into God's powerful arms.

Back to Craig's story. As he and I were talking about his life and his father, I tried to get him to talk about his faith. It quickly became obvious that because of the stress that he felt from his teachers, coaches, and father, Craig couldn't separate their expectations from his understanding of God.

He thought God, too, must be disappointed in him. He presumed that God demanded even more of him than anyone else. I tried to help him to see that Christ had called him to live as a child at play, but I couldn't get through. As far as I know, Craig still sees God as someone who doesn't understand him or who genuinely cares about him. To this day, Craig's life is anything but an abandoned romp of adventure and faith. Like most people, Craig has settled into a black-and-white life of performance and expectations, of duties and obligations, living only for the weekend.

That isn't the life Jesus Christ came to bring. In fact, it's exactly the kind of life God came to rescue us from.

BIBLICAL FAITH

SEEING LIFE AS A GRAND ADVENTURE MAY SOUND NAÏVE TO SOME. For these people, the Christian faith is about knowing the right things about God and doing what's morally correct in light of revealed truth. While it sounds right and proper on the surface, this view of faith—limited to knowledge and behavior only—softens and even weakens the power of redemption in Christ. God wants your son to live beyond mere morality and to see life as a risky, wonderful, exciting, and energizing adventure. This deeper and more biblical understanding of faith is what so many of us lose as we get older. But as dads, we can't lose sight of childlike faith. The gospel is certainly about this kind of radical abandonment to Jesus Christ and his truth. It is not about trying to live inside prescribed boxes of cultural Christianity. Take, for example, the words of the apostle Paul:

> I consider everything a loss compared to the surpassing greatness of knowing Christ Jesus my Lord, for whose sake I have lost all things. I consider them rubbish, that I may gain Christ and be found in him, not having a righteousness of my own that comes from the law, but that which is through faith in Christ—the righteousness that

comes from God and is by faith. I want to know Christ and the power of his resurrection and the fellowship of sharing in his sufferings, becoming like him in his death, and so, somehow, to attain to the resurrection from the dead.

Not that I have already obtained all this, or have already been made perfect, but I press on to take hold of that for which Christ Jesus took hold of me. Brothers, I do not consider myself yet to have taken hold of it. But one thing I do: Forgetting what is behind and straining toward what is ahead, I press on toward the goal to win the prize for which God has called me heaven-ward in Christ Jesus. (Philippians 3:8-14)

At first glance this can sound like spiritual martyrdom— "I want to share in his sufferings." That's how many people view their faith: "For now I must somehow 'press on' in my Christian commitments, meaning I will hang in there going to church, singing songs, evaluating sermons, writing checks, and perhaps even serving on a committee or in a ministry." Our sons aren't immune from this kind of defeatist spirit, for it's what they see modeled by Christians all around them.

I believe this is one of the greatest weaknesses in the church today. We live as if Jesus Christ came to earth, died and rose again, and has been taking a nap for two thousand years, but telling us to hang in there until he wakes up and comes back. We've lost the vibrancy and expectation of his living Presence and his imminent return. We've reduced our faith to a series of right ways to think, but forgotten about pursuing right ways to live. And we've been teaching our sons, at least implicitly, to follow in our mud-caked footsteps.

But look at the passion and vitality of Paul's words:

- I consider everything a *loss* that I may *gain Christ* . . .
- I want to *know Christ* . . .
- I *press on* . . .
- *Forgetting* what is behind and *straining* . . .

A friend I was sharing these thoughts with remarked, "This sounds like a theology of works to me, which is what you fight against, Chap." But my friend missed the point here. As fathers, we *must* remain fixed on the goal of faith—Jesus Christ, and him alone—and make certain that is the message we pass on to our boys. I contend that the reason we see so much of the Scriptures as "doing" and performance is that we've been indoctrinated with this ethic. And we fail to see the vitality and passion behind the familiar rhetoric. The bulk of the passages that describe God's intention for us while living on the earth reveals an entirely different perspective from the one most believers experience. Paul doesn't offer even the slightest hint that it's an option to simply "hang on" in mundane ritual or stale, stuffy religious activity. In Christ, your son is called to a vibrant, organic, and passionate adventure of trust in the living God. He's to *live* his life in Jesus with a vitality that's impossible apart from the true hope of the gospel and being empowered by the Spirit of God. On his journey, your son is compelled to consider as rubbish (or literally, dung) anything that would hold him back from grabbing Jesus' hand and going after life with sacrificial, childlike abandon. Paul longed to "know Christ" and to "press on" until the finish line. This is the gift of faith we have to offer our sons. To offer anything less is to rob them of the spark of the Spirit and the intent of the gospel message.

Okay now, how does a father instill this kind of faith in his son? There are four areas where we can help our boys to see life as a grand adventure: help them to recognize this basic understanding of faith, expose them to the wonder of God, create opportunities of risk and adventure, and teach them to listen to their God.

#1—Holding Fast to the Truth

It's hard to come up with a list that will make this happen. Helping your son experience his faith by seeing life as an adventure rather than a checklist is more about spirit and attitude than action plans and activities. But that doesn't mean you can't take some practical steps to plant this foundation within your son's soul.

First, whenever you deal with issues of faith, ground every discussion and moral question within the context of *relationship* rather than *principle*. God cares about people and he cares about your son. Of course, God is also concerned with behavior, but the *motive* for his concern is his compassion for people. God knows that all morality ultimately comes down to how people respond to him as King. He knows that the final point in all ethical issues is who we trust.

For example, consider the ethics around your son's attitude and behavior regarding sexuality. As you lead him, try to frame every discussion in terms of the grand adventure of God's creation. Instead of drawing arbitrary boundaries (like the ratings of movies) or tossing out adult-like platitudes ("Just Say No"), discuss sex from a relational point of view. Talk about why God created sex, what a wonderful gift it is, how the misuse of our thought life and our behavior can hurt people. Let your son know that, like any powerful gift, sexual fixation and activity has an incredibly harmful side when we allow ourselves to dabble with it outside of its design—a committed love relationship confined to marriage. Let your son know, for example, that lust is dangerous because it destroys our ability to genuinely care for a woman when we let ourselves use her in our minds. When we ignore God's Word in this area, we break his heart, because he knows that we're designed to trust him for our deepest longings. Selfish sexual ambitions rob us of that focus, and we take others down with us.

It's not what my son *knows* about faith that will transform him into the kind of disciple that will change the world, but rather what kind of life he lives. If I see my job as trying to get him to go to church every week, read his Bible every day, and memorize a certain number of verses, I run the risk of robbing him of the *reason* behind each of these. The means or tools of our faith don't matter in the end. What matters is the vibrancy of our faith. I need to be more concerned that I occasionally catch a glimpse of that sly, "Man, is this terrific stuff!" smile when my son thinks or talks about God. Then I'll know he's on the way toward setting the world on fire for Christ. Few have that kind of passion today, *for anything!* Those who do are like beacons in a dark, lonely wilderness. This is the difference between living a life of impassioned abandonment and living in stress and fear. This is the difference between adventure-living and a "duty dance." Help your son choose the truth of an impassioned, abandoned, adventuresome life.

#2—Knowing the Wonder of God

The goal of any discipleship strategy is to develop within our sons a passion for God. But what does this mean? How do we guide our sons into seeing life as a grand adventure where they display an authentic, inside-out passion for God?

Passion can't be controlled, ordered, taught, or manipulated. It comes from deep within. I may know it when I see it, but it's hard to grab hold of or even talk about. Think for a minute—what gets you up in the morning? What stirs your passion, especially for God and his kingdom? Obviously, we dads must first do some tough self-analysis before we can even begin to move on this with our boys. Still, I'm certain most adult believers who hold fast to Jesus Christ could locate an internal place where they feel some level of passion for Christ. This passion, then, is an essential element in our son's development as a mature follower.

Passion begins with exposure to something wondrous, something that captivates our hearts and stirs our souls. It may be a song, a story, or a sunset. From there, when the wonder has the time and space to settle into us, it produces a sense of awe. This is the moment when we hear, "God really does love us, huh, Dad?"

As we cultivate and nourish the awe, we find ourselves experiencing brief moments when we sense a spark or a small flame of something beyond ourselves, something compelling and inviting. Finally, when we allow ourselves the freedom and the environment to fan that spark, it begins to glow into a fire of passion.

Like any fire, the more we feed that spark, the more potent the flame. A person who blazes with abandoned passion is someone who has felt and tasted God in his gut. This is the kind of faith Paul was talking about in Philippians 3—a life of intense, inner passion for God and his kingdom.

To help your son experience the wonder of God and his revealed love, there are two specific practices to implement in your leadership of him. *First, regularly expose your son to creation* while grounding that experience to God's self-revelation to him. Just *going* camping or fishing or skiing/snowboarding will never be enough. You need to augment these experiences. On a chairlift, ask your son to consider how God made the snowflake. On a walk, consider a weed and a flower, and talk about God's idea of beauty. When you're camping, stare at the stars, and talk about God's majesty. The point isn't in these ideas; it's in your ability to connect the dots already inside your son so he sees that God is magnificent and he is all around us.

Second, avoid pat answers, particularly once your son hits age ten or so. Struggling intellectually with the apparent inconsistencies of faith or various paradoxes of life are great tools to drive us back to the mystery of our God. Some parents are afraid that encouraging our kids to question their faith and to wrestle with tough issues will damage them. But the reverse is true. Allow your son to deal with arguments against the faith that he'll eventually be exposed to anyway; this will let him know that this struggle is a *good thing.* I'm not talking about filling his head with philosophical apologetic conclusions and ready defensive responses for those who disagree with him. Rather, I'm encouraging you to let your son struggle to the point where he's drawn back to God as the source of his answers. Your goal is that, at a young age, he'll learn that God is the holder of the answers, so we need only to trust him.

#3—Living the Adventure of Risk

Your role in instilling in your son a faith marked by trust in God is to create the environment where he can discover and explore wonder, cultivate awe, and ignite a spark. As he's led to grasp that God is powerful, mysterious, and wild, he must be given the opportunity to flesh this out by experimenting with that truth. Encourage him to take risks for his faith and to see that true life is found in the adventure of risk.

Most fathers hate the idea of risk. Adventure is fine; just build in safety. Don't ask us to allow our kids to take chances, to go against the flow, to risk. But there is no *real life* without risk. Yes, life is unsafe in so many ways. But is a sheltered, controlled, and ordered life really any safer than a adventurous life of faith? I'm not advocating doing unsafe acts to experience the fullness of life in Christ. I am not really talking about "acts" at all. Rather, the environment we're called to create involves a risky faith unique to our individual sons.

Last summer we watched (notice the choice of wording) our then nineteen-year-old son, who a few weeks earlier had broken his leg playing rugby, go to East Africa for the summer with three or four seminary students to serve the poor in Kenya. He didn't ask us if he could go; rather, the previous fall he informed us of his plans for the summer. He made the decision, he wrote the letters, and he arranged the trip. We were a bit nervous about his trip (okay, we were scared to death!). But we were also incredibly thankful God would call him to do something radical in faith on his own initiative.

Without negating the power of his experience, just let me say it was so much more than we could ever have dreamed for him. In our best moments of planning and strategizing our son's faith development, we could never have produced what God did in and through Chap's decision to spend the summer in Africa. Our best move through all of this, frankly, was to stay as uninvolved and neutral as possible. This was his trip, his dream, his passion. Our job was to fan the spark, doing whatever we could to empower his vision.

Risk will look different for your son. But I'm suggesting you work hard to stay on that edge. Taking a year off before going to college may sound crazy to you, but for your son it may be the best thing he ever does. Empowering his desire to tutor a kid across town may be a logistical pain for your family, but it just might be the best energy you ever expend. What he does will not matter as much as creating the environment where he's free to take the plunge of risking out of his love for God. This is real living.

#4—Learning to Listen

Most fathers complain that their sons don't listen to them. But that's because we have it backward. As we're leading them to view God as intimately safe and entirely faithful, *we're* called to be listeners. Listening is a powerful relational tool. If you commit to being physically present and if you listen with undivided focus, your son will eventually believe that you actually care about him—what he thinks, what concerns him, and how he sees and experiences life. This may be tough, especially at first; we've been conditioned to think our role is to direct and define our sons' lives. But if you maintain a steadfast commitment to "wasting time" with your son, you'll soon find places and opportunities to connect with him. As his trust in you progresses, he'll begin to trust that you indeed have his best interests at heart, and you can season your listening with words and messages of encouragement to trust God like a little child.

FROM FATHER TO SON

1. The next time you have even a brief conversation with your son, tell him a story about a relational or faith risk you took that made a difference in your life. Make sure you communicate the negatives of the risk as well as any positives and lessons you learned.

2. Tell your son about the story of Craig, the stressed young man I wrote about at the beginning of this chapter (you don't have to confess that you got it out of a fathering book). And ask his opinion of that guy's attitude. Try to draw out your son to talk about life as a grand adventure.

3. Ask your son to describe something he thinks would be adventurous, and make it possible for him to live it.

4. Find a way to experience creation in a way you don't normally. Perhaps take a walk together late at night (after bedtime, so he feels you're getting away with something), or take a hike in a new area, or perhaps even roam in a corn field (if you're from the city), or watch the city lights from a hilltop (if you're from the country). As you are out together, read Psalm 19 and talk about how big God is and how tremendous the gift of creation is.

GO FOR IT!

Because authentic passion comes from the inside when your son is exposed to something (or someone) awesome and majestic, take him on a trip (for a day or more) where he'll be exposed to something entirely new. What you do may be uncomfortable, challenging, beautiful, or disturbing. But just having the opportunity to broaden his exposure to the world can provide the environment for you to bring new insights about who God is.

FROM FATHER TO FATHER

1. Talk to each other about a time when your faith could be called a grand adventure. How did you feel? What were the circumstances? Discuss how things have changed (if they have) or what you're doing to keep that spirit alive in you now.

2. Most fathers would agree that risk is a frightening thing for dads. Most of us don't want our sons to take risks; or if they do, we want them to risk *safely!* But risk is an essential element of faith. Share with each other how you

feel about your sons seeing faith as an adventure that requires risk.

3. Ask each other: "What kind of listener are you as a father?" How do you think your sons would answer that question? Cite some recent examples and pray for each other.

PART III

FROM FATHER TO SON:
PASSING ON REAL FAITH

How We Walk Alongside Him:
A Father's Role in His Son's Faith Journey

I like to compare the job of a father to that of a long-distance runner. Fathering isn't a sprint—it's a marathon. It's a long and often trying journey. And, like the marathon runner, we must have disciplined hearts if we hope to successfully finish the course.

—KEN CANFIELD

NOW THAT WE'VE LOOKED AT THE MARKS OF A DISCIPLE AND THE goals of discipleship, we're ready to think more completely about our role in the discipleship process of our sons. Perhaps this is the logical place this book should have started—the doing of discipleship is probably what brought you to the book in the first place. But this design was intentional; I wanted you to think through both what your son's life should be like as well as what you are aiming at as you lead him closer to Jesus. Now that we've struggled through the essence of what it means to follow Christ authentically, our role as fathers has a context to operate in.

This last section, however, may be difficult for you. It requires you to examine your own faith and life as you focus on guiding your son. The first two sections may also have elicited sobering thoughts and emotions, but this section is undeniably pointed. If you don't authentically walk with Jesus Christ, or if you're inconsistent in the way you live your faith, treat your wife, or deal with your son, this section will be almost impossible to appropriate. I'm not saying this to frighten or discourage you, but to remind you of what I said in the Preface. Discipleship is primarily a life-on-life adventure of traveling together on the journey of faith. If there's any issue or area where you know you're not living a life that reflects the faith you're hoping to pass on, I encourage you to get help from someone you trust— a friend, a pastor, or a therapist. There's no shame in seeking out help in your journey. In fact, it's a sign of strength.

This section contains three chapters. Each one offers specific issues that can make or break a father's attempt to encourage his son's faith. They may not contain the kind of advice you have been looking for or expecting from a book like this. But the issues comprise the day-in-and-day-out life you face with your son. In these real and pragmatic areas, you'll win the right to model and to speak into your son's life in God's name. As you read, please don't try to fit everything I say into your son or family system. Instead, consider how the issue works itself out in your family. This will ensure that you can truly touch your son with the love of God.

One last thought: As you continue reading, keep in mind what I've said over and over in different ways and which is *especially* important for you as you finish this book: You're one of the most important and unique figures your son's life; clearly, you're the most influential man he'll ever know.

This may sound intimidating, but with it comes an undeniable blessing from God himself. Of all the people your son will meet and connect with, you are the one man he will always long to be close to. Your son not only needs you, he also wants to know you, to love you, and to please you. God created us with this drive. In this lies your comfort, and it is the one truth that can sustain you in the darkest and most desperate days of your relationship.

CHAPTER 10

ENCOURAGING UNIQUENESS:
HELPING HIM TO BECOME HIS OWN MAN

O LORD, you have searched me and you know me.
You know when I sit and when I rise; you perceive my
thoughts from afar. You discern my going out and my
lying down; you are familiar with all my ways. Before
a word is on my tongue you know it completely, O
LORD. You hem me in—behind and before; you have
laid your hand upon me. Such knowledge is too wonderful for me, too lofty for me to attain.

—PSALM 139:1-6

WHEN YOUR SON WAS BORN, DID YOU HAVE GREAT HOPES FOR him? Did you buy him a mini-football to celebrate his coming into the world? Or a guitar, book, or CD?

I remember holding my sleeping one-month-old during an exciting college football game and whispering how much fun it would be to watch Notre Dame football together. He had the ND beanie, the bib, and the pennant. He was right next to me that entire first season, cheering the Irish on to another mediocre season. But the score didn't matter—my son and I were going to enjoy this *together,* for a lifetime.

You probably guessed it. He is now a committed Pac 10 fan, especially loyal to the University of Southern California, one of Notre Dame's archrivals. When fall arrives, our friendly banter quickly becomes a hotly competitive discussion. I'd raised him—I thought—to love what I love and to appreciate my perspective on life. But as he got older, I realized that somewhere along the way he took a turn from my way of thinking and became his own man.

A few questions for you about your son:

- What do you want him to love to do?
- What do you dream for him?
- What do you expect out of him?

When your son is young, this kind of dreaming and planning comprises some of the most wonderful and exciting moments of your life. If you're a sportsman, of course he'll be a sportsman. If you love the outdoors, naturally he'll love the outdoors. If you are good at math, he'll become an engineer. If you're into classical music, that passion is sure to rub off on him. And if you love God, enjoy old hymns, and like to listen to contemporary Christian radio, then it's only natural that your son will follow suit, right?

If you're a dad who has been down the road a ways with an adolescent son, you've already begun to recognize that your dreams for your son have not necessarily jibed with his dreams for himself. Maybe you've already experienced that bloodstained battleground where the dreams, desires, and expectations of a father meet head-on with the differing dreams, desires, and journey of a son. If this is hitting a little close to home, that's okay. It's normal! This is a regular fear and frustration of being the father of an adolescent son.

If you had a checklist to describe the desires, dreams, or hopes you had for your son when he was young, which of these words would you use?

- Plays musical instrument (Which? What kind of music?)
- Is a reader and thinker
- Plays sports (Which sports? What position?)
- Loves music (Types?)
- Likes computers and techno-gadgets

- Likes the outdoors
- Likes to write
- Is a sports fan (Which sports? Which teams?)
- Is a singer
- Is active in others lives (ministry, service, etcetera)
- Fixes things (cars, house, etcetera)
- Leads other people
- Has a few close, intimate friends
- Is a free spirit
- Is a math and science guy
- Is funny

These characteristics, interests, and activities are fine in themselves, but only if your son chooses them from within. As committed fathers, we should try to expose our sons to options, opportunities, and activities but then encourage them to make the ultimate choice.

SOME STORIES TO PONDER

PHIL'S FATHER, AN ELDER IN HIS CHURCH, LOVED TO PLAY JAZZ SAX-ophone. By middle school, Phil was better than his dad. But in ninth grade, he stopped taking saxophone lessons and took up playing bass guitar, over his father's objections. He got an earring and a small tattoo and started playing bass in a local punk band. He soon quit going to church. Phil ended up dropping out of high school to tour with his band for a small, Los Angeles record label. At nineteen, his lifestyle and his fully tattooed arms and torso caused his father to quit speaking to him.

Glen loved to sing and act, but his dad was an officer in the local youth soccer association. Although his father attended church and it was important to him (when it did-n't interfere with a scheduled game), his first love was the game of soccer. Glen's dad coached, so Glen played most of the games, even though other parents complained that he hadn't necessarily earned his spot on the team. He tolerated the sport to avoid conflict with his dad. Secretly intimidated by his father, Glen hid his theatrical dreams, and avoided any kind of relationship with his dad as well. In high school he was cast in a lead role in the school play. But his dad, secretly disappointed that Glen had "turned his back" on the sports lifestyle he loved so much, was "too busy to come" and watch the play. Now thirty years old, Glen is a singer and dancer in small theater, and he hasn't had a meaningful conversation with his father in years. He lives alone and survives on odd jobs. He never goes to church. "It is irrelevant," he now glibly claims.

Shawn was raised a Christian, involved in Sunday school and youth group. Shawn's dad was a deacon in their church and his family was the proverbial "perfect Christian family." But Shawn knew a different story. His father, an objectively good guy, led the family in a strict regimen of family devotions and Bible reading. His intent was to "raise up" Shawn as a godly son who would be committed to Christ and an equipped leader in the church.

Shawn's entire life was filled with conversations and reminders (for example, posters, books, tapes) that he was "special to God." Shawn's dad insisted on family nights together and praying together as a family. But in normal, everyday life there was no focused exposure to his dad's heart of faith or any passion for God outside of religious family duties. As Shawn went through junior and senior high school, he struggled with the rituals of faith having any real meaning in his world. When he tried to talk to his dad about his feelings, his dad would either give him a simplistic "Sunday school" answer to his questions or they would fight. Shawn is now just out of college, is a well-liked man and passionate rugby player, lives with his girl-friend, and feels sorry for his parents because they are "slaves to the crutch" of religion.

These three boys—Phil, Glen, and Shawn—have walked away from the faith of their fathers. Three boys who wanted to be noticed, listened to, and valued for who they were as growing, vulnerable adolescents. Three fathers who were so consumed with what they wanted for their boys that they missed their sons. Three fathers who now daily have to face themselves in the mirror and ask, "What went wrong?"

THE PAIN OF LETTING GO

IT HAPPENS TO EVERY MAN, AT SOME LEVEL AT LEAST. HE KNOWS he *must* say good-bye to his child-son, yet it can be so hard. You're reading this book because you care about your son. My word to you, then, is that you have what it takes to love your son as Christ has called you. But you must also be aware of the issues you're going to face as you love your boy. You are his greatest fan and his hero. In the letting go, know that you're helping him grow from a floundering, dependent boy into a fellow lover of God and others.

The most difficult part in this is that the boy we must say good-bye to remains in our world. I'm not talking about the actual good-bye when you embrace him after setting up his college dorm room or see him off for the military or new life elsewhere. That's tough, too, but it actually comes later. I'm speaking of the good-bye when your son takes those first few steps on perhaps the loneliest journey of life—when he ventures out into adolescence.

Few adults recognize the precarious nature of adolescence. For the first time in his life, a boy intuitively recognizes that he needs to move on from the part he has played up until this time—the role of a child. Until now, he's been dependent on his family, specifically his parents, and the security that comes from being surrounded by stable and caring people. Even his faith, though it may have elements of maturity and depth, is somehow intrinsically linked to these primary relationships. But childhood doesn't last forever.

Somewhere around eleven or twelve, he begins to change. Certainly physically—he gets taller, bigger, a deeper voice—but in subtle ways as well. He stops being so free with his passions. He's moodier and at times more distant. Obviously, temperament and family norms make a big difference in how he expresses these changes, but every boy at some point begins to assert his desire to break free from the bonds of childhood.

To parents, this process can look and feel like dismissal or even betrayal. Once your son climbs up the pole of childhood and steps off the platform onto the tightrope of adolescence, he has no choice but to go it alone. His intent isn't to wound or reject his parents, or even to separate from them, although his behavior can look like it. In a world without rites of passage or rituals that help a young man navigate from one stage of life to the next, he's simply taking the next developmental step in the best way he knows how. He's just as confused about this process as you are. The bedroom door becomes a significant boundary of protection during this time, as do the stereo, phone, pager, and computer. In just a few years, an increasing distance often develops between a father and son as he enters adolescence, and it's usually hard on the whole family. During this time the point of greatest strain is in his relationship with his father.

In the three stories mentioned earlier, each boy took steps during adolescence to assert his need for independence to develop a unique identity, and none of them wanted to make an intentional break from his dad. Each son wanted his father to recognize and appreciate him for who he was, or at least for who he was becoming. Each father couldn't handle his son's seeming rejection of what he hoped for. Phil (the bass player) never had the love for saxophone that his dad dreamed for him, although he had learned a love for music. When he switched instruments, in his disappointment his father pushed him away. Glen (the actor/singer) never felt he fit with either sports in general or his dad in particular, although he did learn to passionately commit to something else he loved. Still, Glen's dad never seemed to notice how far away from him his son felt. Shawn was looking to incorporate his father's faith into his developmental journey, but his dad never invited him into the inner room of his belief in God, so Shawn went his own way. He now takes his divinely driven passion for life into the only thing he believes can bring him fulfillment—his friends, rugby, his girlfriend. Yet Shawn can't see that God offers him the greatest passion of all in Christ. He's a great kid who can't seem to connect his zest for life with the Christian faith as he experienced it growing up.

To this day all six of these men wonder what happened to the life and faith they once shared.

As fathers, we go through a variety of feelings as our sons grow up. This often affects our ability to be objective about the choices our sons make for themselves. The first step is to recognize how hard it is to let go of the hopes and dreams we have for our sons and to recognize that they are not our creation; rather, they're God's creation, made in his perfect image.

WHAT A FATHER FEELS

AS THE WALLS GO UP AND THE QUEST FOR INDEPENDENCE GROWS, subtle changes take place in the family system. This begins to upset the entire family balance. "You're not being your-self" is a common parental mantra during the adolescent years. As a way of trying to bring back what once was, a father may remind his son that he always used to like to play this family game or watch this show or go shoot hoops in the park. You may have enjoyed a relatively stable relational environment for the entire life of your son. Until now, he's been an integral member of the family and a part of you. At some level it hurts most dads to watch this transformation, and it's incredibly frustrating to have no power to do any-thing about the changes your son is going through.

When I told my friend Greg I was writing this book, he actually grabbed my arm and said, "Are you going to talk about how hard it is to let go?" His oldest son—his "best friend"—was showing signs of pushing him away. Greg didn't yet recognize that the push was not against him but against the role of "child" in the family. Greg feels like he is losing his son, but he knows that there is something strangely normal and even necessary about the process.

That doesn't mean he likes it, and he surely doesn't know what to do with his feelings of frustration.

What Greg feels is precisely why the process of adolescence must happen. A boy can't be a boy forever. Because our society is no longer going to clearly mark the path to adulthood with training, nurture, and celebration, most sons figure a way to forge a path for themselves. Fathers (and mothers and other caring adults) can be and need to be there for their boys as they grow into men. But for your son the trek toward independence and maturity is lonely. In keeping with the tightrope metaphor, modern adolescence is the process where a child becomes an adult by growing independent as a person (adolescence) while preparing to function in a world where he must be interdependent in community (adulthood). He's never called to give up dependence, but spiritual maturity means he learns to transfer his dependence from his family to God.

In today's society, this process can be wrenching, for by definition adolescence is a self-focused time of life. Other than infancy, adolescence is probably the most self-centered season of one's life. But don't worry. A vital part of your son becoming a responsible and interactive adult is being comfortable with who he is and how he fits with others. This is why fathers need to remember that parenting is a long-term, marathon-like time of life. In a world where there are few safe places, getting through the process of adolescence is tough for everyone. Some make it through much healthier than others. But along the way, it's hard for every son at times.

During adolescence, your son must make the move—on his own—from dependence on his family to independence to, ultimately, interdependence with others while walking dependently with his God. But *during* this in-between stage, life and relationships and even family are confusing, difficult, and occasionally frightening. When you first see the signs of this new journey, you can be sure your son isn't aware of what he's feeling or doing.

But somehow he knows he must take those steps into the new social and psychological frontier set before him. Throughout the entire process of the adolescent journey, most parents feel they're losing their son. But that's the *last* thing he wants to have happen. He doesn't need his parents less. If anything, he'll need them *at least* as much as when he was just beginning to walk. But what he needs from them looks far different from what most of us would assume.

Over the years, I've become convinced that the lack of a father who cares is one of the most devastating experiences in an adolescent's life. I can cite many studies and statistics that overwhelmingly assert this fact. But it is perhaps more important to reflect on the power of our own relationship with our fathers. We can name men who were unable to be real or honest, who couldn't freely love and honor a woman, who needed to control kids on an athletic field, or who were closed and arrogant in relationships out of the deep sense of loss because of a dad who was not there. This is no secret. But it's easy to miss that a dad may *appear* to be involved, caring, and supportive of his son when his behavior and influence can actually be a constant discouragement to his son's need to become his own man, the man God created and redeemed him to be. There's an important distinction between being *involved* in the activities of your son and being *present* for him in the way that sets him free to grow into God's man.

WHAT A DAD (OFTEN) TRIES TO DO

WHEN A BOY BEGINS TO SHOW THE SIGNS OF ENTERING ADOLEScence—insolence, sloth, sullen irritability, a kind of calculated distancing—the instinct of an involved father is to try to get up there on the tightrope with him and reassure or even "train" him while standing next to him. This is where the fireworks start. Obviously, the timing and intensity of this type of situation depends greatly on a variety of complex factors:

- how a father and son have negotiated their relationship before adolescence
- how much inner strength and real support a son feels he receives from his dad
- how free he feels to be honest with his dad
- the overall support and relationship a son has experienced with his father over the last few years
- a father's ability to encourage and embrace his son's uniqueness

As we saw in the examples of the three dads earlier, the last factor—encouraging and embracing a son's uniqueness—is perhaps the most important on the list. In fact, it's a catchall for the other issues. As a son begins to explore who he is apart from others, his understanding of what's good about his uniqueness becomes the core issue of his young life.

As your son goes through this transition, your natural instinct will be to control him or to distance yourself from him. But what your son really needs is for you to take a much more balanced approach.

#1—The Controlling Father

You've seen it. Maybe you remember it from your own teen years. Or maybe you've already done it to your son. You just want to "be there" for your son. But if you're like most dads, as soon as he makes a slight stumble, you feel compelled to take over. This is probably one of the worst things a father can do. Even a slight move toward parental control or a perception of critique about who a son is becoming will generally cause a powerful reaction that even he doesn't understand. It may be expressed as rage, hiding, or arguing. But the emotion behind distant or even destructive behavior when he bumps up against his dad is most frequently a deep-seated frustration because he knows it's time to go it on his own. This is normal, right, and even necessary for him as he grows up into the man God has called him to be.

During this time, an adolescent son longs for two things: First, to be seen by his father as worthy and valuable in his own way; and second, to have the explicit and consistent approval of his father, regardless of his behavior. I'm not saying that dads must be held captive by their sons' longings. Of course, it would be irresponsible to allow our adolescent sons to live without rules and boundaries. But these two longings are what your son thinks he wants. This is the source of greatest conflict and friction in father-son relationships. The longings often collide, especially when a father tries to place restrictions on his son's behavior. It's impossible to approve of everything your son does, but saying *anything* will seem to your son as if you've violated his primary need for unquestioned and unconditional acceptance. For a father who cares about his son, the adolescence process is a tough journey. You want to be his fan, but you must be his protector and life trainer. In his journey, he'll want to please you, but not at the expense of his drive for autonomy.

On top of all of this, the son's internal struggle to find himself often looks to the father like a simple lack of maturity, gratitude, and/or appreciation. This can often cause dads to offer such helpful and reconciling platitudes as "at least you have a father who *cares!*" An over-involved father, or one who refuses to recognize that his role in his son's life needs to change as he grows, can stifle the process and in the end actually do more harm than good for his son.

Herein lies a vital axiom of life as a father: A son needs to know that his dad likes who he is, even while he is only on the journey to get there and the process is far from complete. It takes prayer, finesse, patience, and compassionate emotional stability to walk the balance of support and accountability. The controlling dad throws in the towel and tries to call the shots in his son's life. This may work for a while, but in the end your son will either walk or run away.

Instead, you need to stay firmly in control of the *process* you're both going through. It's up to you to prayerfully rise above the petty yet potent emotions that will divide you.

Instead of saying something like, "You don't know how lucky you are," your attitude needs to constantly communicate, "No matter how frustrated I feel, I am and will always be your greatest fan. You may not know it now, but someday you'll be stronger because I've been in your corner."

#2—The Distant Father

Some men move the other way when their sons take the first few steps toward independence. A father's reaction can often be pictured on either end of a continuum—from a "He's growing up now and he needs his space" attitude to a "Fine! If he wants me to leave him alone, I'll leave him alone—I'm done" attitude. Both of these represent a father's unwillingness to be present for his son the way his son needs him to be present. He may be a great father, but when a young man begins to spread his wings and "play adult" around the junior high years, the father who gives too much space or flat-out rejects his son, due to his changing behavior and attitude, denies his son the dad he needs so desperately through this period.

A son can give grace and can handle a dad who is consistently distant, as in a divorce situation. But a father who is either so consumed in his dreams for his son or who is what psychologists call "technically present but functionally absent" can be very hard on a growing boy who keeps looking for ways to get his father to love him for who he is.

This is even worse for a Christian father, for usually a son will consider how his dad treated him to be a model of how God will treat him. This is one of the main causes of uninvolved, spiritually distant Christian men in our pews. They were raised by distant fathers who never blessed them for their uniqueness and quest for independence.

In the heat of battle, this can be incredibly tough for a dad. Sometimes running away, even if only emotionally or relationally, shouts to your son that his behavior and attitude can cause you to turn your back on him. Most fathers don't *intend* this message, but a father's withdrawal or stoic distancing can't help but say to a son, "I can't handle you.

You're on your own." If you *must* back away because you are too emotional or aren't in control of the process, then certainly do so, *but only for a season!* Then make sure your son knows that you simply need some space and that you're frustrated and don't want to hurt him.

Yes, Dad, it's hard sometimes not to say our piece and then flee. We often feel taken advantage of or abused—or even deeper, like failures. We find ourselves at a loss as to how to connect with our sons, especially during those times when they are going off on their own. But because you love your son and because you're his father—God's love-gift to your boy—you owe it to him to be a man who can stand tall, even when you don't feel like it. Buck up and fulfill your calling as his hero, his fan, and his consistent anchor. Resist the temptation to step away or hide. Seek out other dads to pray with. Invite your wife and closest friends to tell you the truth and to teach you how to match your personality and temperament with your calling. Most of all, *don't* let yourself forget that God created you to be your son's father, and he's given you all the resources you'll ever need to hang in there and love your son.

#3—The Balanced Father

What a balance dads have to maintain! On the one hand, many times it seems best just to let your son be, encourage him in his quest for uniqueness, and hope he safely figures life out. On the other hand, your son will make such poor choices, play a role that's clearly not representative of who he is or wants to be, or have such an immature grasp on life that you feel love demands you to step in and make sure your son stays safe and moving forward on that adolescent tightrope.

But *both* reactions can actually hurt your boy. Letting him be leaves him dangling when he's thoroughly unprepared for the complex and dark world he's attempting to navigate. But wresting back control keeps him from going through the life experiences he needs to become a unique man of God. I've bounced back and forth between these two behaviors with both of my boys for years. I'm well aware that I've hurt them in both ways. There must be a better way—a more appropriate place to stand—than jockeying for room on the tightrope or leaving the arena, hoping he doesn't fall.

That's why you're reading this book. During adolescence, you must be a father who, with your wife alongside you (if possible), stands *below* your son, looking up, holding onto a safety net, calling out words of encouragement, offering advice when he's ready to receive it—all the while intent on watching your son walk *alone* across the tightrope of adolescence. This is a weighty and sometimes disheartening position for a father, especially one who deeply cares about his son. You want to walk with him and sometimes *for* him. You want to help him avoid falling and to tell him when and how to take that next step. But the role he needs you to play involves subtle coaxing, gentle persuasion, and occasionally just standing ready with the net when he takes a step that you know will cause him to tumble or slip. Your role has changed when your son takes off on the adolescent journey. You're now the supportive guide, the respectful coach, and the understanding and concerned older friend. And you're still his father.

This is a difficult and delicate balance to maintain. But love offers us no alternative. On the one hand, you must watch out that your son doesn't hurt himself or others as he makes "adolescent" choices. As he grows and seeks his own way and own space, you need to learn to negotiate with him so he has the best shot at growing into an independent man of God. Ultimately, you want him to be able to decide how to make good choices, to love God from the inside out, and to be light and salt for Christ in the world.

As he's growing up, it's your job to work with him to define what he should control and where you need to maintain absolute parental authority. Nearly every parent-teen issue has room for negotiation. Issues like curfew, bedtime, the use of the phone or computer, and even his choice of friends all provide a tremendous laboratory for your son to safely learn what it means to become his own man. When he violates an agreement or takes advantage of his negotiated freedom, certainly you should step in and calmly and compassionately tighten the reins a bit. Even here, the wisest move you can make is to include your son in deciding the consequences of his actions. Remember, your goal is to present your son to Jesus Christ as a mature man, responsibly committed to love as a disciple. You have only a few years in this lab, and it is a golden opportunity for you to work with your boy as he learns to make his own decisions, lives with his own consequences, and charts his own path before the God who loves him.

Throughout this process, it's vital that you maintain your relationship with him. Most often the rub will be where his will collides with yours. It generally comes down to the difference between a father arbitrarily imposing rules and boundaries and a father and a son recognizing and agreeing on legitimate boundaries. When your son was a child, you could force him to live by your rules, simply because they were the rules. But parenting an adolescent is about helping him to recognize that life has *real* rules and *real* boundaries. The freedom to make choices is an important part of growing up, but violating the law, hurting others, or being flippant or arrogant toward life violates God's eternal boundaries.

A father who desires to lead his son to God must be careful not to allow too much freedom for the sake of family peace and not to allow too little freedom in the name of protection. A father who loves his son will work hard to communicate boundaries clearly, will give flexibility and room for choice within those real boundaries, and will provide appropriate consequences for violations. This father will make room for dialogue and negotiation, but he'll also be careful not to acquiesce to a son's argument for full freedom and boundary-less adolescence.

If you haven't yet been through this stage of life, it sounds just a bit daunting, doesn't it? Remember that God loves both you and your son. Trust God, be humble with both your Lord and your son, and keep the goal in mind: leading your boy to his own mature relationship with Christ. You will find God to be faithful and sure as you walk through life with your son. God is building your boy into the man he created him to be. Rest in that truth as you concentrate on being God's instrument of love and nurture.

FROM FATHER TO SON

1. The next time you and your son have a conflict, ask him for his solution to the problem. Maybe it's time for a compromise or a new level of trust. If his solution seems appropriate, just smile and say, "Go for it, son. If I can help you, let me know."

2. Ask your son to tell you the last time he felt you wanted him to be more like you than like himself. Asking questions, try to see how you can repair what has been done. And ask forgiveness.

3. When your son begins to show his independence from you, instead of resisting him or jostling (or even outright fighting), honor his statements.

GO FOR IT!

Listen to and watch your son for an indication of something that may be uniquely him. Examples may be a new sport or activity, trying out a musical instrument, or participating in a ministry opportunity. Surprise him by doing the legwork it takes to give him a shot at trying it.

FROM FATHER TO FATHER

1. Try to remember some of the dreams you had for your sons when they were little. What about now? Are they living up to what you wanted for them? Reflect with other dads on where these dreams are good and where they may be keeping your boys from exploring their own lives.

2. Share with each other the biggest single source of conflict between you and your sons. Help each other to brainstorm strategies for handling these and still honoring the developmental growth of your boys. Pray for each other.

3. Discuss together the idea of "negotiating boundaries." Where, specifically, do you think this is appropriate in your individual families and where do you struggle with this idea? Help each other to experiment with a "baby steps" approach to being flexible in this area.

CHAPTER 11

AVOIDING
THE "DO NOTS"

A son's experience of his father, whether it is one of absence, neglect, presence or abuse, is a powerful one and directly impacts his sense of himself as a man and as a father.

—TED BOWMAN

JEFF IS TRYING TO BE THE BEST FATHER AND HUSBAND HE CAN. HE leaves his house early each morning and generally comes home about seven. This means that for more than half of each twenty-four-hour day, he's involved with his work. He has three kids, two boys (fifteen and twelve) and a girl (nine). Jeff's an assistant coach for both his younger son's and his daughter's soccer teams, which means he leaves work early twice a week for practices, goes to as many of his older son's games during the week as he can, and his Saturdays are booked with multiple games. Jeff's wife also works and, being a compassionate guy, he sometimes makes dinner (or at least is in charge of the cleanup), goes to the grocery store, helps out with homework, and tries to arrange his schedule so he can take his kids to the doctor or chaperone field trips. Even though he gave up having his own life a long time ago, he occasionally slips in a round of golf or a few days of fishing. But when he does something for himself, he has a hard time shaking the guilt. On Sunday the family goes to church, where Jeff teaches a fourth-grade Sunday school class, and spends the rest of the day catching up from the busyness of the week.

Do you ever feel like Jeff? Do you sometimes feel too busy to rest, your life too full for meaningful interaction with anyone? Are you too tired to even take the time to ask these questions? Even when we think we're doing everything the world expects of us, we're somehow reminded that we're not quite as on top of life as we ought to be. Maybe it just comes with the packaging of postmodern fatherhood, but it does seem as if a father needs an army of voices around him keeping him on his toes. Whether it is . . .

- the look of annoyance on his twelve-year-old daughter's face when he fails to hang in there during her detailed description of her day
- his wife's need to continually remind him that he needs to call the bank *today*
- his son's cold shoulder when all he tried to do was find out how practice went

It seems a dad has a hard time finding a win, even in his own home. Can you identify with that?

I wonder how many of today's fathers have simply run out of the gas they need to be the kind of "nurturing dad" they know they're expected to be. I'm guessing that sometimes you feel that if you go to the games, bring home a check, are somewhat involved in church, and are basically a nice person, you're doing the best you can as a father. Of course, it's when you're feeling this way that you have even fewer emotional and physical resources to take the hits that can come with living with kids.

Still, we know that there's more to this fathering thing than doing the expected activities. We're called to be encouragers, caregivers, and co-nurturers in our kids' lives. Maybe there are some guys who have parenting so wired that their kids have no problem listening to them give advice or knowing the definitive signals regarding when to leave dad alone with his paper. Maybe their kids freely give them the benefit of the doubt no matter what they say or do. But then there are the rest of us. Generally, the word on the street is that guys are rotten communicators and even worse interpersonal relaters. Taken to extremes, this line can allow us to justify disengaged selfishness or flat-out boorish, arrogantly detached behavior.

But remember, the Bible doesn't give us any wiggle room on this one. Men are created in the image of God, and God is relational. As men and fathers, we were created for intimate, caring, active relationships, *period!* Men remain called to be aware of and ready to give up any attitudes and behaviors that may imply we are better than or separate from any other member of our family. In today's world, many of us fathers carry the tendency to slip into roles that are uncommunicative, authoritarian, or distant. But this is not how God intends us to live.

That's precisely the point of this chapter. Throughout the centuries and across cultures, men have created social systems that allow them to behave in any way they want. Yet the vast majority of admonition and encouragement in the New Testament offers no hint that men are to be the distant providers and protectors and women the nurturers of the children (this cultural stereotype, however, has crept into our theology). When it comes to parenting, men and women are called to care for, nurture, be kind to, and respect their children.

I believe that as we concentrate on what it means to parent and spiritually nurture our sons, we'll be better men as both husbands and fathers. I also believe that as men take on the responsibility to love and cherish their kids, especially during those formidable years of adolescence, they'll recognize that their role is equal to that of their wives.

It's rather amazing that the only times the New Testament talks directly about how parents should deal with their kids, the father is always the subject. It only occurs twice (in Ephesians 6:4 and Colossians 3:21), but it's worth noting that there's not a word in the New Testament telling mothers how to parent. Dads are singled out. So, apparently, there's something about fathers that we need this kind of direct . . . um . . . encouragement.

IT'S ALL ABOUT COMMUNICATION

LIKE IT OR NOT, WE LIVE IN A SOCIETY THAT HAS EFFECTIVELY taught men how to be lousy communicators, *especially* with those they love. Most marriage counselors will tell you that the most common issue hindering marital bliss is a lack of healthy communication between husband and wife. While not always the case, the ultimate responsibility for a breakdown falls into the guy's lap. As men get older, they tend to fall into patterns that further hinder communication, and this almost always leads to many other sorts of relational issues that take a great deal of time and energy to undo. But it's simplistic at best and theologically reprehensible at worst to blame this on the fundamental makeup of the male personality and temperament. Men, in their hearts, know better.

There probably are many ways to demythologize the male stereotype that states that we as a gender-community are simply incapable of clear, fair, honest, compassionate, and kind communication. But there are two that tend to keep me falling into the "I can't help it; that's the way men are" trap. First, while the Scriptures tend to imply that some subtle and necessary innate differences exist between men and women (other than those that are culturally defined and prescribed), the clear intention of God in both creation and redemption is that we are far more alike than we are different.

> In the image of God He created him; male and female he created them. (Genesis 1:27)

> There is neither Jew nor Greek, slave nor free, male nor female, for you are all one in Christ Jesus. (Galatians 3:28)

The image of God is by its very nature relational. In his essence God is a loving relater, first with himself in the mystery of the Trinity and subsequently in his desire to bring his people into the intimacy of his triune community. If we say we are created in his image, we must then be infused with the intrinsic desire and need to be in loving, intimate community—men as well as women. A theology of creation redemption demands that men recognize that we are every bit as called to intimate, open, warm, honest, and real relationships as women are.

The second way that keeps me from distancing myself from those I love is to remember that, although today my default position may be to shut down, retreat, or hide from intimacy and relational work, I have not always been that way. Very few men, when they were dating and falling in love with their eventual spouses, pulled in the shutters and fled behind the remote control. Romance that culminates in marriage takes hours and hours of late-night talks, strolls in the twilight, passionate and exhausting debates over simple things, and deep soul-searching and penetrating honesty in resolving conflict. Deciding to cast one's lot with another for life is no small task. And nearly every man had to dig down deep to live up to the relational demands of the journey. The seed of the ability to connect at deep levels is still there, ready to be watered and nurtured to vibrancy.

What does all this have to do with being a father? Everything! Especially when we recognize that who we are matters more to our sons than who we're trying to make them be.

AVOIDING THE "DO NOTS"

THE TWO PASSAGES OF THE NEW TESTAMENT THAT PROVIDE DIRECT warnings to fathers are:

> Fathers, do not exasperate your children; instead, bring them up in the training and instruction of the Lord. (Ephesians 6:4)

Fathers, do not embitter your children, or they
will become discouraged. (Colossians 3:21)

Both of these passages are sandwiched between advice to children (obey your parents) and slaves (obey your masters). They provide snapshots into an important yet simple list of issues that the apostle Paul felt needed to be mentioned. Where are the words to mothers? Evidently, mothers didn't need encouragement to watch their attitudes and behavior in the same way fathers did. The list touches everybody else in the household, including wives, and the words are fairly cut-and-dried (submit, love, obey)—until it comes to men. Then Paul gets more specific in calling us to be proactive with our behavior, first with our wives ("do not be harsh") and then with our children ("do not exasperate" and "do not embitter"). As fathers who care about our sons, we're to avoid these two responses toward our boys.

Because these two words are related and yet slightly distinct, a careful look at each is important. "Exasperate" comes from the Latin prefix *ex,* which adds intensity to the following word, and *asperare* means "to make rough." The Greek word *parorgizo,* "to provoke to anger," is a rare word that suggests a strong emotional reaction to some word, attitude, or action. Here it means that a father must avoid any type of behavior that will incite in his son a strong, angry reaction. This was radical teaching in the first century, as Craig Keener notes:

Children were often taught through beating, which
was standard in child rearing and education; fathers
were considered responsible for their education.
Paul is among the minority of ancient writers who
seem to disapprove of excessive discipline.[3]

In my circle of friends who are fathers, we asked each other when we had exasperated our sons and what we had done to provoke such an emotion. We decided that it usually had to do with one of three things: the way we talked to them, treated them, or held our power over them. The most common word we used was that we "frustrated" our sons to the point of anger. And the more we talked, the more we recognized we could do a better job of preventing this kind of reaction.

The best way I can describe how a father may exasperate his son is to confess my own failures. I've hurt my boys and violated this principle repeatedly for years. I regularly exasperate both of them, and yet I long to do better. Because I'm convinced that almost every dad violates this fundamental precept of fathering, as you read this list, ask yourself when and how you have exasperated your son. Here is where I have blown it with my boys:

- I've continued to push my son when I've already made my point.
- I've been, or at least have appeared to be, interested in the bottom line, the win, or the grade more than in the process of growth.
- I've asked more of my son than he's capable of handling or comprehending.
- I've allowed myself to be careless with sarcastic or even mildly degrading humor.
- I've used poor timing in trying to guide and correct my son when his greater need in the moment is for support and encouragement.
- I've been more interested in information or logic than in trying to understand what he's going through in life.

It's no fun to publicly admit my failures, but to do so often takes me onto the most significant growth edge as a father. If I hope to help my sons recognize that God is a loving Father who has called them into a lifelong adventure of trust in him, I need to make sure that the way I treat them doesn't stand in the way. The New Testament doesn't give me any other advice. It's as if God is saying to Christian dads, "You want to create an environment for your son to discover and experience me? Get out of the way! Treat him with respect, love, and tenderness. Correct him with great care, and appropriately discipline him with specific and clear reasoning. Do what you can to affirm his basic manhood. Then . . . step back and watch me work."

But I know that many times I've stepped in and exasperated my sons. One of my sons had been having a hard time with a teacher and was not doing too well in the class. I wanted to be there for him, to help him, and to "encourage" him to do whatever it took to pull the grade up. My intent was noble, but my method was pathetic, because I couldn't separate myself emotionally from his responsibility. My son needed to learn this lesson himself, but I had a hard time letting him make his decision. He ended up doing fine, but in the meantime we often got into heated arguments that were almost totally unnecessary. I just couldn't let go. I still struggle with this tendency and, in the name of love, I'm involved in their lives. But I do little good when I exasperate them in my enthusiasm.

Like "exasperate," "embitter" involves provoking to the point of anger. But to embitter someone is to provoke an internal reaction. "Exasperate" is usually exemplified in an external angry reaction, which we can at least recognize and address. But to embitter our sons is to "cause sharp pain or discomfort." The Greek word is *erethizo,* which has to do with provoking strife and contention. Keener describes this as Paul again making a case for "a more gentle approach to child rearing."[4]

The second phrase in Colossians 3:21 helps us to recognize the force of Paul's argument: "Do not embitter your children, or they will become discouraged." If we want to encourage our sons, we need to avoid making them bitter. Bitterness sows the seeds of discouragement, the exact opposite of what we want to give our sons.

Again, to best illustrate this I need to confess where I have embittered my own boys. This list, like the last one, isn't exhaustive, but it clearly shows how far I have to go as a father who longs to disciple his sons in Jesus' name.

As you read this list, consider your own fathering style, how you come across to your son, and what you do to slip into embittering him in a way that causes discouragement.

- I've not taken the opportunity to connect relationally with my son.
- I've not taken the time or effort to understand my son.
- I've shown more interest in my son's performance—scholastic, athletic, or even church—than in his life.
- I've had a hard time apologizing when I was wrong.
- I've demanded respect but have not always respected my son.

Considering this list of failures makes me feel rotten. But I also feel I must make progress toward growing out of these attitudes and behaviors. Dee and I have been talking for some time about the different ways I exasperate and embitter our sons. Oddly, she can say *exactly* the same thing I do, even with the same tone of voice, yet she doesn't elicit even close to the same reaction.

There's something between a father and his son that is unique, especially through the adolescent years. We're the ones who need to be honest, teachable, and open to changing our behavior. It's up to us to heal the breaks, to take the first steps of reconciliation, and to be aware of how we come across to our sons. I encourage you to ask your wife (if you're married, and if not, ask the mother of your children) where you both exasperate and embitter your son. She'll be glad to refine the list I have only started for you. Then the real work begins.

FIVE STRATEGIES FOR AVOIDING "DO NOTS"

IN MY LIFE AND MINISTRY, I'VE DISCOVERED FIVE STRATEGIES THAT go a long way in helping fathers *not* exasperate or embitter their sons. Of course, there are no guarantees, for the dynamics of adolescence are varied and complex. But because these five are grounded in a solid theology of fathering and encompass most of what we've already addressed in this book, over time these will serve you well.

#1—Be *for* Your Son

Remember that the most important thing your son needs to know is that you are for him. You're his biggest fan. Growing up is a marathon, not a sprint. Your goal is to provide an environment for your son that encourages him toward living in a committed relationship with Jesus Christ when he is an adult. A major piece of this is your son's relationship with you. He must know that you're there for him, even when he's not there for you. He must sense that you want to be close to him, even when he's pushing you away. And he must believe that you care enough about him that you're willing to do the hard work it takes to build bridges of communication with him, no matter how long it takes. This will allow him to experience the unconditional and stable love God has for him and in far greater measure. Be your son's greatest fan, and let him know that, win or lose, solid play or major league error, you'll *always* be his fan.

#2—Listen to His Reasons

Recognize there's a reason for everything. Your experience, history, and age make you fairly dangerous when dealing with your son, because most of us tend to think that we actually know everything about everything. So, when you come up against a potential conflict or rule breach, or a request that you deem unreasonable, or any other attempted power negotiation, it's too easy to fall back on your instant and infallible fatherly wisdom. However, when you do this, you'll not only relationally cut off your son, you'll usually miss his side of the issue. Your son deserves the respect of a complete hearing, and when you genuinely understand his viewpoint, you'll not only honor him, you'll build confidence in him as well.

#3—Stay Calm

Staying calm and emotionally caring but freely objective is a great way to honor your son. I often allow myself to get emotionally involved in my boys' stuff (what my therapist wife calls "enmeshment"). This regularly causes me to commit one or more of the mistakes that exasperate *and* embitter them. One strategy to avoid this is to take a step back, say a prayer, remind myself that I love my boys— *before* I head down the road of panic.

Every man is different, and each of us needs to be as honest about our ability (or inability) to stay calm when we want to blast away at our sons. But no matter how competent you think you are, I want to encourage you to *consider* that you may actually be human and you're subject to blowing your cool at times. The most helpful advice I have ever received came from an elderly woman who knew me well. After she observed me dealing with my kids, she said, "Just ask Dee how calm you are." That clinched it for me, not because Dee was a therapist-to-be at the time, but because she was my wife, and she knew me better than anyone else. I know that a lot of men chafe at the idea of inviting their wives into the "holy of holies" of their behavior. But, face it: who else can tell you the truth—if you're open to it? Ask your wife to help you to see when you dance on the edge of losing your cool.

#4—Ask Questions

Do your best to ask questions and really listen before you jump to conclusions or give advice. I'm notorious for making hasty judgments or quickly offering unwanted counsel, especially with my boys. I have this disease that causes me to have a knee-jerk reaction to most issues they experience. But when I take a breath and calmly ask questions, my sons are far more likely to allow me into dialogue with them so that we both can see what we need to deal with.

I know few men who are good at asking questions. Most of us are good at giving advice or at diagnosing someone else's problem. But to ask good questions and then, naturally, to *listen to the answer,* is a rare male talent indeed. But you really have no option here—your love for your son (and your family, and even your friends and coworkers) compels you at least to be adequate in this area. What got my attention here is when a friend thanked me for some of my sage advice, and then tore into me for not having the slightest idea of the context of his issue. It is simply a fact: Without asking good questions and being a thoughtful listener, you will always do damage to the process of leading your son as a follower of Jesus.

#5—Communicate Without Attacking

Communicate your disappointments honestly without attacking your son. "I feel frustrated by what looks like lying" deals with your perception of the behavior in a way that leaves more room for discussion than "You lied to me!" The key to this is to not imply intent. Once you go down the road of claiming to know your son's motivation without allowing him the opportunity to identify and see the best course of action or error of his ways for himself, you'll immediately cause conflict, defensiveness, and exasperation. But sharing with your son how his words or behavior have affected you or others is a great way to create an open and honest exchange of perspectives between the two of you.

As you lead and love your son, remember that God has called you to be as much a nurturing presence in his life as his mother is. You're not only capable of this type of relationship with your son; you've been created for it.

FROM FATHER TO SON

1. The next time you catch your son being "exasperated" or "embittered," step back and take a spiritual time out. Ask God to reveal to you whatever you've done to contribute to how he feels. Sit down and confess your actions to him and ask his forgiveness.

2. One of the major reasons we exasperate our boys is because we ourselves are somehow exasperated. The next

time you feel yourself getting angry with, or losing perspective toward, your son, emotionally and spiritually step back and confess your angst to the Lord. When you reengage with your son, ask questions and listen to him.

3. When you find a teachable moment with your son that isn't rushed, show him the two verses in this chapter: Ephesians 6:40 and Colossians 3:21. Tell him you want to be the kind of dad that takes these passages seriously, and invite him to help you. Talk with him about the meaning of the words "exasperate" and "embitter." Ask him to pray for you, and invite him to let you know when he thinks you're causing him to feel these things.

GO FOR IT!

When a conflict arises between you and your son, go through the checklist in this chapter: Make sure you're for him, listen for his reasons/thinking, stay calm, ask questions, and communicate without attack. Make this is a standard checklist. Put this internal filter into play every time you experience, or even anticipate, conflict.

FROM FATHER TO FATHER

1. Share with each other how you feel given the expectations of fatherhood today. Is it relatively easy for you? Are there any areas where you feel bitter, used, or taken advantage of? Talk about how this affects your fathering of your sons.

2. In your own words, define the two keys words from this chapter: "exasperate" and "embitter." Describe what they look like in your sons. Confess the behaviors or attitudes in you that trigger these types of responses in your sons. Pray for each other.

3. Consider: In what ways is your life so busy that you don't have room to breathe, think, and be careful in how you treat your family—especially your sons?

CHAPTER 12

A FATHER'S ULTIMATE CALLING:
TO LOVE HIS PRODIGAL

There is no need for fret when faithfully turning to Him if He leads us but slowly into His secret chambers. If He gives us increasing steadiness in the deeper sense of His Presence, we can only quietly thank Him. If He holds us in the stage of alternation, we can thank Him for His loving wisdom and wait upon His guidance through the stages for which we are prepared. For we cannot take Him by storm. The strong adult must become the little child, not understanding but trusting the Father.

—THOMAS KELLY

WHAT IS OUR "ULTIMATE CALLING" AS FATHERS? THOMAS KELLY has it right, recognizing that "the strong adult must become the little child." We're called to love the boy that God loves so much and to teach him to love his God with the abandon of a little child. How do we actually *do* this?

For decades we've believed that the answer to raising up young people as authentic disciples of Jesus is to provide education and programs. For you as a father, is it enough to love your son to Jesus by participating in Christian programs and events?

Cliff loved the retreat, but something about the time bothered Barry. Cliff had been on the point for his church in designing and implementing a father-son retreat. He'd read about it, discussed it in his men's group, and received encouragement from the pastor to work with the junior high intern and "go for it." The idea was to take the junior high boys and their fathers into a wilderness setting to initiate them into manhood by following the models of rites of passage from other cultures.

Cliff and his team decided that the way to welcome boys into manhood was to take them through a demanding obstacle course with the dads shouting encouragement and spurring them on to keep going. They found some old bear traps and other massive outdoor tools to enhance the rugged nature of the experience. After this, they orchestrated an evening ceremony by the fire where each dad would tell his son (in front of everyone else) that, as of now, he was to think of himself as a man. Then the dads prayed for their sons, broke into teams for a late-night game of Capture the Flag, and drove home Sunday morning in time for church.

Cliff felt like it had gone great. His son, an eighth-grade athlete, told his dad it was fun and thanked him for the weekend before putting on his Walkman and falling asleep. Cliff was pleased with himself—his dream had gone well.

Barry's son, a smallish seventh-grader, hadn't enjoyed the weekend. Cliff's son and a few other older boys had picked on him most of the time, and he didn't feel he had done well on the obstacle course. Several of the kids (with the lighthearted encouragement of some of the dads) made it into a competitive thing, betting on who would win and who would be the slowest. Luckily, Barry's son finished in the middle of the pack, but he'd felt the pressure to do well.

He'd also had a hard time with the ceremony of blessing, where the men publicly said things about their sons. He was embarrassed because his dad said things he hadn't ever said to him, and he wasn't even sure what his dad meant by much of it. To be called a man now seemed like it should feel good, but he knew nothing had really changed. He was still a kid, especially to his dad. While trying to come up with something meaningful to say at the ceremony, Barry—sensing something was wrong—backed off from his true feelings in mid-thought. Flustered, he ended up cracking a joke about his son's room. On the way home, Barry felt awful, and his son refused to talk.

Two dads, two experiences, and one programmatic event aimed at providing a ritualistic experience to propel a group of boys from childhood into adulthood. Did the event live up to its expectations? Can such an event—or any program for that matter—produce a son committed to an intimate, abandoned relationship with God that will flourish for a lifetime?

This "rite of passage" type of event is picking up steam in the fathering movement, especially the Christianized version. These events try to recreate other, mostly ancient rituals to facilitate a boy's entrance into the fellowship of the men. But what's rarely mentioned is that those rituals followed a years-long and specifically prescribed litany of training and rites that prepare both the son and the community for this shift in status. What was seen as a powerful culmination following years of apprenticeship and preparation is now being reduced to a brief and superficial event that makes the men feel they've done something for their sons. And the boys feel generally positive about spending time with their dads, even if they have no idea what they just did. With thoughtful and trained leadership, this type of event *can* be a great step in deepening the relationship between a father and his son. But, at best, it's simply another program designed to bring fathers and sons together. But a program, even the most well-intentioned one, can't be the primary means by which your son is led into a vibrant, passionate life in Christ. There needs to be something more foundational, more intimate, for him to truly grab hold of the faith of his father.

As I attempt to close this book by summarizing the *how* of leading our boys to authentic faith in Christ, the first question to ask is, What does it *mean* to raise up a "godly" son? Or, better, what does a "godly" son look like?

WHAT DOES A "GODLY" SON LOOK LIKE?

THIS QUESTION IS IMPORTANT BECAUSE IT REVEALS THE GOAL. ARE we trying to raise sons who look, talk, and appear to be "godly"? Or are we out for something different? This is a crucial question. After reading a book like this, most dads may still want to get their hands on a prescribed list of activities or ideas that will offer visible, tangible, and quick results. As much as we will try to hide it from ourselves, we want to *see* results. As much as we acknowledge that true and lasting growth is a long, slow process, most of us need some markers that tell us we are on the right road. We want to feel that our ministry to our sons is "effective." The problem? It has to do with the question, What do we mean by a "godly" son?

I've given you a hint about what I think by putting quotation marks around the word "godly." After all, everyone wants to look like they have achieved a certain level of spiritual maturity and to be declared godly. But the way the Bible speaks seems to make this issue fuzzy, because sometimes the words seem to suggest the opposite—for example, when Paul declared himself to be "worst of sinners" (1 Timothy 1:16). Still, there's a strong perception that if I'm to develop a young man sold out to the truth, then being *seen* as godly is the most important characteristic in my son.

There are two reasons "looking godly" can be a negative, or even harmful, goal. First, in my experience the idea of being a godly person is often a superficial descriptor at best, especially when talking about a boy in the midst of his adolescent journey. But even for adults, the harder we strive to be godly, the farther we seem to tumble, behind closed doors, from that ideal. I'm afraid that when we labor to develop our sons into men who look and act godly, we foster an outside-in, exterior, and dualistic attitude toward faith. This inevitably produces an inauthentic faith that is more about pleasing people than pleasing God. For your son, *true* godliness is something that begins, develops, and eventually is manifest from the *inside* of him.

The second reason "godly" is in quotes is that the Bible does not support it as a true test of discipleship. The word itself is far less common in the Scriptures than we'd guess. From the way many people talk about the Christian experience, being godly is right at the top of the list. But in Scripture, "godly" is most often used *descriptively* of someone who is intimately related to God. It almost never refers to something we're *prescriptively* called to strive for. Sure, your son should strive to live a life that reflects who he is by God's grace. But the Scriptures also proclaim that even when he makes mistakes or goes through a tough season, as one who has been accepted by Christ and who has called upon him, your son is still included in the list of the godly.

The truly godly are those whose lives have been so captivated by Jesus Christ that this relationship *incrementally* produces the fruit of the Spirit: love, joy, peace, patience, kindness, goodness, faithfulness, gentleness, and self-control (see Galatians 5:22-23). These character qualities then begin to spill over into others' lives. The Bible refers to those who have been shaped by an authentic, abandoned, internal faith as "godly." As your son displays an aspect of the fruit of the Spirit—when he is kind or shows self-control—that's an observable marker that God is at work in your son. Those are the markers of his authentic "godliness."

SO, WHAT HAPPENS WHEN I'M DISAPPOINTED IN HIM?

I'VE LIVED THROUGH ENOUGH WITH MY BOYS AND HUNDREDS OF other developing young men that I'm sure of one thing: A man on a quest for intimacy and abandoned trust in Jesus Christ will disappoint those who love him. Your son will be selfish; he'll fall, he'll lie, and he'll possibly even renounce his faith. There will be moments when he's right on track, with an observable growth in his relationship to God and others. Then there will be times when he falls back into behaviors and attitudes that convince you he has barely started the journey. As his father, your son's up-and-down faith journey may drive you wild. But the key you must always remember is this: Faith is a *journey.*

When my sons have disappointed me and when I've allowed myself to forget everything in this book, I find myself identifying with my friend Roger. Roger's son, Conner, almost sixteen, came home on fire for God from a mission trip to build homes for the poor in Mexico. He and Roger had been praying together for years, and Roger had tried to keep his cool over his son's apparent lack of enthusiasm for his faith. But this trip seemed to make up for years of discouragement for both Roger and his wife. They swelled with pride and parental satisfaction after hearing Conner tell the entire congregation of his renewed faith. They wept when he offered to help around the house, was nicer to his little sister, and even read his Bible before going to bed. Their son was finally on track with personalizing his faith.

Two weekends later while on a business trip, Roger got an emergency call from his wife. She was hysterical. Conner had sneaked out of the house after coming home from a movie, and even though he had no driver's license, he'd taken Roger's car. Roger was understandably incensed. He canceled his meetings, took the next flight home, and was fired up by eleven o'clock the next morning when Conner finally woke up. Without asking questions or hearing Conner's side of things, Roger sat him down and let him have it. During his tirade, he allowed the most destructive words to a child's faith journey to come out of his mouth: "I guess all that talk about God in Mexico was just a lie, huh? How *dare* you lie to those people in church."

What about Roger's anger? Clearly justified. Should there have been confrontation and discussion around such themes as lack of trust, a violation of their relationship, and abuse of freedom? Certainly. Are consequences, potentially severe, warranted? Absolutely. But ridiculing and questioning an adolescent's experience of faith and condemning his courageous public stand for his relationship to God can be significantly damaging to both his faith and his relationship to his father.

When Roger and I talked about this, he was still so emotionally charged by his son's failure and breach of trust that he blasted his son when talking to me. As he spoke, I remembered a few times when I'd felt the same way toward my boys, even if I'd never come out and verbally assaulted their personal faith. I felt a deep but penetrating pang of guilt. At this point, sitting there listening to my friend go on and on about how mad he was at his boy, it hit me. Both Roger and I were so disappointed in our sons' behavior because we're disappointed in our own failures.

When my son fails or slips up, my anger comes from my own inability to understand or forgive myself. If I'm honest in those times, I'm actually more disappointed in myself and scared for my son than I am truly disappointed in him. At some level deep inside, I feel like I'm a fraud and that I'm anything but godly. I hold on to those times when I have let my Lord down, when I have made stupid and selfish choices—and I have a hard time believing that my faith is as authentic and committed as it appears. I get mad at my son's failures because I'm mad at my own. How can I possibly help my son be "observably" godly if inside I struggle to believe it for myself?

As I reflect on the truth of the gospel message, it's not *my* godliness that matters. What does matter is what God wants to do in my life and how I respond to that. This is the key to helping my son see himself as a growing, truly godly man. It's not his *consistency* that makes him a disciple; it's his willingness to honestly and openly confess his need for the Lord to make him into a godly man.

The next time you're disappointed in your son and find yourself angry, the first gut check for you is to figure out the source of your anger. Is it fear for who he's becoming? Remember, the journey is a long, winding road. Is it because you know you're fully capable of a similar failure? Confess this to yourself and to your God before you get anywhere near your son. He desperately needs you to be able to rise above the immediacy of the issue and be his father.

WHAT DO YOU DO, DAD?

WHAT HAPPENS WHEN YOUR SON BEHAVES IN SUCH A WAY THAT you feel he doesn't reflect the godliness you long to see in him? Or what happens inside your soul when your boy acts just like any other kid? Or what happens when he does something that's such a reversal of what you'd been seeing that your world feels rocked from its foundation?

What happens when your son seems to be doing pretty well but then turns around and gets drunk, uses drugs, gets a D, has a few bad friends, or gets involved sexually with that sweet little freshman from the youth group? What happens when you feel like your heart has been ripped out by your son? Where do you go with your feelings of anger and fear and frustration and disappointment? Who hears you scream, or cry (if you're healthy enough), or yell and bang things (if you're not)? How do you control your emotions and remember that he's on an arduous journey of both life and faith?

I speak to you as a father who experiences all of these things and more. I'm a dad who has been in Christian ministry my whole life. I've been a "youth expert." I've doled out advice *ad nauseam* in print, on radio, and in public. I've counseled others on how to understand their children, how to parent, and how to love kids in need. But at the same time, I know I'm as much in need of healing and healthy perspective as anyone I've ever counseled.

I also must confess that a part of me is deathly afraid to even admit this. I'm worried about what you will think of my boys. I'm concerned about what you will think of me as a father. I'm nervous that I'll be found out, that life is not as simple and clean as I (and so many others) have made it seem in the course of books and lectures. Yet the time has come and I am compelled to tell the truth to fathers out there who have no place to go with the pain of disappointment and failure. You, my friend, are not alone if you've ever seen your son make a choice that doesn't reflect the faith you're attempting to pass on. In fact, you're incredibly rare if you've never experienced this with your son.

THE ONLY HOPE WE HAVE – LOVING OUR SONS AS GOD LOVES US

I'M SITTING IN A BORDERS CAFÉ TYPING FURIOUSLY WHILE IMPLORing the Holy Spirit to use my pain and experience. Whether or not you have experienced the heartbreak of being disappointed in your son, his behavior and choices—and therefore in yourself—the gospel offers us oh-so-human dads hope, even in the most dark and lonely of days.

The best way I can offer hope in caring for our sons as the Father loves us is to come back to the life, character, and teaching of his Son. The way Jesus loved, the way he treated people, the integrity and self-discipline that controlled him—these are the characteristics I want as I walk with God in a way that is a beacon for my sons. Perhaps the most pointed description of how God loves us is found in the parable of the prodigal son.

Every person goes through many prodigal episodes in his life. We inevitably don't trust the Father, and we go out in search of life on our own. We all make stupid and dangerous choices. We walk away from responsibility, ignore authority, and take life into our own hands. The especially disconcerting truth is that we all will continue to do this as long as we are human and call this world "home." This tendency toward rebellion has dug its claws deeply into our psyches. And as deep as our faith may grow, we're never far away from the lure of the darkness.

Throughout your son's journey of faith, remember that no matter how far he falls, no matter how inconsistent he is, no matter how rebellious he seems, he's actually not much different from you. This isn't always easy to admit. But if we long to create an environment and relationship where he feels the Father in our touch and hears God in our voice, it's vital that we do admit it. The parable of the prodigal son gives us the tools and tips we need to love our sons as God has loved us.

There are five decisive moments that occur for the father in this parable. I believe they represent a father's role in doing what he can to love and honor his son during his process of owning his faith and growing into manhood. As we come to the end of our time together in this book, may these tools be a guide for you as you navigate the difficult waters of encouraging your son's process of growing up to be like Jesus Christ, the author and perfecter of his faith.

#1—Listening

> "There was a man who had two sons. The younger one said to his father, 'Father, give me my share of the estate.'" (Luke 15:11-12)

The story begins with the younger son approaching the father with a request: he wanted his half of the inheritance so he could go and live his own life. To every Middle Eastern ear in Jesus' original audience, this request was not only grossly inappropriate, it was also an almost unforgivable offense. Under no circumstances did the son have any right to make such a request of his father.

But the father didn't respond according to the temporal values of his culture. He listened to his son and heard him out.

I find it hard to listen, especially to my kids. A few years ago I wrote a book about rites of passage as a tool in raising sons.[5] In it I recounted the story of my oldest son trying to tell me something early one morning. I was engrossed in my cultural quiet time—the sports page—when he finally ripped the paper right out of my hands and shouted, "Dad! Are you *listening* to me?" My courageous son was so aghast that I was reading the paper when he was trying to talk to me, because he knew I was in the middle of writing a book on being a Christian father. His method may have been a bit over the top, even for an eighth-grader, but he'd nailed me.

Although it's not the main point, it's clear from the way Jesus told this story that the prodigal's father was at least a competent listener. In fact, he was such a good listener that we don't even know what he said or if he spoke at all in this part of the story. It doesn't matter, for his son was the initiator of the conversation, and the father was a caring, careful responder. He somehow recognized that his son had clearly made up his mind over the future course of his life (this is obvious in the next few lines of the story), and he heard his son's decision.

This is perhaps the hardest part of being the father of an adolescent: the willingness to allow enough room for my son to explore life on his own, even though I'm quite certain that if I leave him to his own desires, he'll somehow mess up. To listen, to really hear, is to grant your son the dignity and respect deserving of a man, while not forgetting that he has a way to go before he truly is a man. To listen provides an opening into a world where his dreams, ideas, and passions are taken seriously. The prodigal's father somehow knew this—and so he listened to his son's request.

#2—Resourcing

"So he divided his property between them."
(Luke 15:12)

Have you ever stopped to consider how bizarre the father's reaction was? It's one thing to allow your son to make a decision you think will turn out poorly. It's quite another to freely participate in the decision by funding it. This father did what his son asked him: he divided the estate and let him take his money and head for the big city.

This is the hardest part of the parable for me. It's pretty clear the father knew what would happen. Yet he let his son go anyway. Not only that, he actually made it possible for his son to squander his wealth.

I find this inconceivable, for I've been trained to

believe that if I can somehow manipulate my son or squelch his rebellious or even harebrained dreams or plans, I'm being a good parent. And, in most cases, this seems to be the proper thing to do. When it comes to safety, I have an *obligation* to protect my son from anything that's clearly beyond the scope of what he can handle alone. To say that this parable calls for an "anything Johnny wants" parenting style is to miss the point entirely. Your son needs clearly defined, developmentally appropriate, and maturity-driven boundaries. I believe that the prodigal's father was not funding an immature, ill-conceived philandering for the sake of wild experimentation or adolescent rebellion. He knew that, for whatever reason, his son had made the choice to go his own way, and at this stage of his life the father had to let him go. Every dad knows there are those issues and moments where our son has made up his mind and our best course of action, as painful as it may be, will be to let him step away from our control. As your son is growing in maturity and responsibility, he needs appropriate, negotiated rules and subsequent consequences.

The prodigal had made a decision to intentionally insult his father by denying his own place in the family. He was willing to cause indescribable cultural embarrassment, not to mention wrenching heartache, for the sake of going his own way. His father somehow knew that his son had already made his decision. Out of love, he was willing to allow his son to head in a different direction. This is where we don't know enough, because we don't know how sure the father was that his son would return. But the lack of words speaks loudly as well. He loved his son enough to give him the opportunity not to come back.

What does this mean for a father committed to encouraging his son's pursuit of God? I think we miss a beautiful truth if we reserve this way of thinking only for major, "to the city" types of rebellion. In fact, it's a much more powerful lesson to consider resourcing my son's desire to head in his own direction in the little things. Take going to church, for example. From the time our sons were in high school, we allowed them to make their own decisions about going to church, and even which church to attend. At times this was very risky and even painful, for sometimes our boys took us up on it. But by the time your son is fifteen years old, if he hasn't decided that church holds anything for him, forcing him to go may do more damage than letting him stay home. Encourage him, yes, and even communicate to him why you want him to choose to go with you. But sooner or later, he has to be the one to make the choice.

This is what I mean by resourcing your son's choices. You don't go overboard by buying him kegs for parties or letting him spend the night out every Saturday. You simply let him know that his faith is *his* faith. The prodigal's father understood his love enough to allow his son to go. That illustrates God's love for us, and that's the point Jesus was making. This is also an empowering statement for your son, because he'll hear that you honor his ultimate choice enough to allow and even support his often inconsistent and difficult choices along the way of his journey.

#3—Being a Watcher and a Waiter

"Not long after that, the younger son got together all he had, set off for a distant country and there squandered his wealth in wild living. After he had spent everything, there was a severe famine in that whole country, and he began to be in need. So he went and hired himself out to a citizen of that country, who sent him to his fields to feed pigs. He longed to fill his stomach with the pods that the pigs were eating, but no one gave him anything.

"When he came to his senses, he said, 'How many of my father's hired men have food to spare, and here I am starving to death! I will set out and go back to my father and say to him:

Father, I have sinned against heaven and against
you. I am no longer worthy to be called your son;
make me like one of your hired men.' So he got
up and went to his father." (Luke 15:13-18)

In his classic book about this parable, *Return of the
Prodigal Son,* Henri Nouwen presents a beautiful description of the heavenly Father's posture of waiting and watching as we as his children come stumbling down the road
toward home. The human father in this story was both a
watcher and a waiter. He couldn't have seen his son coming back home if he hadn't been a consistent and faithful
guardian of his son's return: "But while he was still a long
way off, his father saw him . . ." (verse 20).

Waiting for your son is one of the most painful aspects
of being a father. While he's off on his own, experimenting, trying life on for size and fit, the role modeled by the
prodigal's father is to stand and wait. Dee and I have experienced many long nights (and some days) waiting to see
the outcome of our trust. Waiting isn't just staying up late
on the night of the prom or on your son's first night out
with the car. It's also the sheer agony of waiting for him—
sometimes for days, or even weeks, to come out of his protective shell of secrecy and busyness. For an adolescent,
the bedroom door is a significant marker of separation, and
sometimes the wait entails waiting for him to come out of
hiding. But we *must* wait, if we're to allow him to become
a man.

This waiting is an exercise in prayer as well as self-
discipline and commitment. Richard Foster reminds us:

Waiting itself becomes prayer as we give our
waiting to God. In waiting we begin to get in
touch with the rhythms of life—stillness and
action, listening and decision. They are rhythms
of God. It is in the everyday and the common-
place that we learn patience, acceptance, and
contentment.[6]

As we wait for the "return home" of our son—to our Lord and to our lives—we find ourselves embraced by the great Waiter, the Father who stands on tiptoe waiting for our return. God *knows* our journey, our walk away, and yet he also knows that waiting is what love demands. We're called to wait for our sons.

Watching for our sons is just as important. I think that if Jesus had used me in this story, he would have explained how, in using my own sophisticated defensive shield, I would most likely have tried to fend off or even ignore the pain of the wait with busyness. This can be projects, television, or even "godly" activities. But when I do this—whether I'm engaged in my own work, my own play, my own agenda, or even the television or newspaper—I stop watching for my son to come home. It takes deliberate patience and focused, stable commitment to be primed and ready to respond when your son comes home and needs your embrace, or even just your presence.

#4—Running and Embracing

"But while he was still a long way off, his father
saw him and was filled with compassion for him;
he ran to his son, threw his arms around him and
kissed him." (Luke 15:20)

Are you able to let emotion flow through you in a way that pours onto someone else? Most of us men have been raised under a dark, sinister cloud, you know. We've been cursed to believe that real men don't do that kind of thing. To be disciplined to watch and wait is one thing—yes, it's indeed difficult to live in a posture of waiting and watching as our son grows up. But to allow the raw emotion of the wait to remain close enough to the surface that it can explode in a torrent of emotion seems way too much to ask of a contemporary father.

But look at this father—the prototypical father, the father who is a picture of the Father each of us has longed to know and hear and touch. He listens, he resources, he waits, and he watches. All the while his focus is on the developmental and relational needs of his son. He knows his son is on a long, arduous, and at times painful journey. He also knows that his son still needs him. And so he watches and waits, prays and remembers. And when his son is ready, he returns for the embrace.

Your son needs to know that when he turns back into your world, you'll be so excited that you'll rejoice with and for him, kiss him, and embrace him as he returns home.

#5—Celebrating His Return

"The son said to him, 'Father, I have sinned against heaven and against you. I am no longer worthy to be called your son.'

"But the father said to his servants, 'Quick! Bring the best robe and put it on him. Put a ring on his finger and sandals on his feet. Bring the fattened calf and kill it. Let's have a feast and celebrate. For this son of mine was dead and is alive again; he was lost and is found.' So they began to celebrate." (Luke 15:21-24)

There's no hint of condemnation or criticism of the son's choice to leave. There's only grateful celebration that he has come home. As the son returns, in this case there's no need for parental imposition of consequences. The choices he made weren't the result of random, childishly impulsive behavior; they were more about adult greed and selfishness. The son made a deliberate decision to go his own way, and therefore upon his return it was clear he'd recognized that his father was loving and kind and that he could go home and be welcomed at least as much as the servants. Depending on the issue, your son's choices and behaviors may need clear consequences, but he must feel his father's embrace through the outer layer of discipline.

As your son takes time to explore options apart from the faith he's learned from you, the odds are that he'll take a season away from you to search on his own for God. For a while, as you watch and wait, the pain and fear will be very close. But you must wait in the hope that what God has allowed you to be for your son will provide the memory that he'll return to your embrace. And when he does, it's time to celebrate!

Make the celebration fit the occasion. In the prodigal's case, the repentance was dramatic, and nothing but the fattened calf would do. But when your son starts opening up about his dislike for "the hypocrites at church," or telling you of his decision to move on to a new set of friends, or revealing that the girl he liked is drawing him away from God and so he needs to break up with her, your celebration may be a long chat, a slow walk, or even a drive out for a meal or a ball game. Celebration is a reconnection and a meaningful rite of passage—for the son who was lost has come home.

FROM FATHER TO SON

1. Buy your son a gift that describes what you think of him — something symbolic that may be silly but that communicates you're his greatest fan.

2. Write your son a letter letting him know that no matter what he does or how he acts, nothing can shake your commitment to him.

3. Write his favorite Christian artist or writer and arrange to get a personalized autograph and a special, uniquely designed message for him. If you have trouble with this, let me know and I'll help you. My e-mail address is at the back of this book.

4. Surprise your son by taking him out of school to go to lunch, play pool or miniature golf, or see a movie together.

GO FOR IT!

Although programs aren't the end-all to drawing your son into an authentic and powerful relationship with Christ, creating significant rituals can provide him with an important handle for remembering whose he is. As you finish this book, I suggest you make a decision to create a unique ritual for you and your son to experience at least once a year. Simply doing something together that you both enjoy and that's out of the ordinary will provide the common ground where he'll know he can always count on you as his friend and dad. Examples of this could be going to a specific college football game every year, or going fishing at the same place and the same time, or attending the same conference together. What you do isn't nearly as important as sharing a ritual that keeps you in a close, caring relationship.

FROM FATHER TO FATHER

1. What does having your sons become "godly" mean to you? What would it look like, especially for your sons?

2. I asserted that one of the primary reasons we fathers get frustrated and even angry with our sons when they fail or make mistakes is because it reminds us of our own weaknesses and failures. Explore this idea with each other. Even if you don't agree with this, what are some ways it might make sense? After you've discussed this idea as an abstract concept, share with each other how you feel when your sons disappoint you. Describe what that experience is like for you and how understanding your feelings can help you be a more loving, caring father to your sons.

3. What does it mean to "watch and wait" for your sons when they are shutting you out or going their own way?

NOTES

1. *Webster's II New College Dictionary,* 1995, s.v. "trust-worthy."

2. Henri J. M. Nouwen, *Life of the Beloved* (New York: Crossroads, 1992), p. 52.

3. Craig S. Keener, *The IVP Bible Background Commentary: New Testament* (Downers Grove, Ill.: InterVarsity, 1993), p. 553.

4. Keener, p. 580.

5. Chap Clark, with Steve Lee, *Boys to Men* (Chicago: Moody, 1991).

6. Richard Foster, *Coming Home: A Prayer Journal* (San Francisco: HarperSanFrancisco, 1994), p. 41.

AUTHOR

Chap Clark, Ph.D., is associate professor of youth, family, and culture in the School of Theology at Fuller Seminary. He is also president of Foothill Community Ministries, committed to encouraging and strengthening marriages and families through the dynamic of authentic relationships. Chap, with his wife, Dee, writes and speaks frequently on parenting and marriage. They live near Pasadena, California, and have a son and a daughter in high school and a son in college.

Chap can be contacted at Foothill Community Ministries, cclark@fuller.edu.

PARENTING BOOKS FULL OF ENCOURAGEMENT AND INSIGHT.

Daughters and Dads

A helpful book for any dad who wants to understand and support his daughter as she gets older.
(Chap and Dee Clark)

Taming the Family Zoo

Does your house sometimes feel more like a zoo than a home? *Taming the Family Zoo* will help you identify the unique personality type for each of your children and learn to adapt your parenting style to them.
(Jim and Suzette Brawner)